# REMAKING AMERICA

# REMAKING AMERICA

WELCOME TO

## THE DARK SIDE

### OF THE WELFARE STATE

Sven R Larson

iUniverse, Inc.

New York   Bloomington

**Remaking America**
**Welcome to the Dark Side of the Welfare State**

iUniverse books may be ordered through booksellers or by contacting:

iUniverse
1663 Liberty Drive
Bloomington, IN 47403
www.iuniverse.com
1-800-Authors (1-800-288-4677)

ISBN: 978-1-4502-4382-7 (sc)
ISBN: 978-1-4502-4383-4 (ebk)

Printed in the United States of America

iUniverse rev. date: 08/20/2010

*To the Founding Fathers of the United States.*
*Their gift to all mankind was a beacon of liberty; and a pathway to*
*freedom and prosperity for all willing to work hard and honor the*
*principles upon which this great republic was founded.*

# TABLE OF CONTENTS

## WHY I WROTE THIS BOOK

Around midnight on June 8, 2010, a large classroom building at a school is set on fire. The arsonists, young men from the neighborhood, remain on the scene as the fire spreads from classroom to classroom, destroying science lab equipment, expensive collections of books and records of a full year's worth of work for the students.

Fire crews arrive on the scene and prepare to start putting out the fire. But the arsonists and their hang-arounds – in all a group of about 30 teenagers and men in their early 20s – are not going to let them do their job. They start throwing rocks and other small, hard items at the firemen, from piles of projectiles they have gathered earlier that night.

The fire was merely an excuse to create a confrontation.

The commanding rescue service officer orders his crews to pull back from the fire and concentrate on containment. He also calls for police back-up. As law enforcement arrives in riot gear the young hooligans concentrate their aggression on the police. Fire crews resume efforts to try to put out the fire, but the attacks from the young rioters overwhelm both police and the fire crews. They all withdraw and let the classroom building continue to burn uncontrollably.

It is not until almost an hour later that the police have force enough on the scene to protect the firemen and their trucks.

The day after, students were supposed to hold a graduation ceremony at the school and say farewell to each other in the classroom building. But instead of a day of joy and celebration they and their families have to witness the remains of yet another destructive act of senselessness.

Where did this happen? In America? Canada? Britain? France? Perhaps in Greece, a country plagued by social unrest recently?

No. It happened in the housing project of Rinkeby, in the north west of Stockholm, Sweden. It was just one of hundreds of arson attacks on schools in Sweden. It was just one of countless examples of socially destructive behavior in a country that for decades was known as a quiet, socially stable role model society.

Sweden is no longer what Americans have known to be. It is a country in decline and decay. The welfare state that American liberals have touted as a template for America's future is crumbling. The very social fabric that the welfare state was supposed to provide is withering away, leaving citizens short-changed and deprived of services and entitlements they were promised would take care of them from cradle to grave.

Every sector of government, from health care to income security, from education to law enforcement, is walking away from its promises to the citizens. In a process that can best be described as a reversed assembly line, the Swedish government is dismantling its welfare state piece by piece, under endless budget pressure, but it is doing so without giving people the chance to assume control over their own lives.

Still paying the world's highest taxes, still being promised lifelong protection by the government, Swedes find themselves trapped between an ever lower standard of living and a government that defaults on promises right and left.

The destructive process is a wake-up call for America. We are moving in Sweden's direction, being promised a welfare state but without being told of its dark, detrimental consequences. Those are on full display in Sweden today.

The youth gang that burned down that classroom building annex to the school in Rinkeby outside Stockholm is a product of the welfare state's defaulted promises. They have grown up in a society where the government promises everything, but delivers less and less. Throughout all their childhood they have seen how a benevolent government turns its back on them everywhere they go.

In school they are treated as cost units more than students. If they need health care, doctors – if they can get to see them – treat them as cost units more than patients. When they cannot find a job and apply for welfare, they are treated as a problem, a burden, a cost unit – not as a citizen in need of help.

I, too, once believed in the welfare state. But having seen its dark side first hand I could no longer support it. I decided to share my story with America. This book tells the story of why Sweden today is a stingy society, run by politicians whose only focus is on how to get rid of the welfare state because they can no longer afford it. But they want to do it without cutting taxes and without expanding freedom in return. This book tells the story of how a welfare state that started out as the citizen's best friend has turned into a totalitarian machine where citizens are problems, not subjects. A machine driven by fiscal fascism.

It is the story of what has happened in Sweden – and what will happen in America, if the liberals that are currently running the country can take just a couple of more steps down the road to big-government. It is the story of the transformation of an entire country from a home of free and independent citizens into a fiscal prison, populated by truncated individuals with no other prospect in life than to depend on an ever stingier, ever more fiscally fascist government.

There is a link between the abstract fiscal technicalities that dictate government policy in Sweden today, and the youngsters that burn down schools, kindergartens, libraries and government-run sports arenas around the country. This link is never mentioned in the debate over America's ever growing government. It is a link that dehumanizes people, first by forcing them to live a life that fits all the entitlement programs that the government provides, then by depriving them of

3

the very same entitlements because the government no longer has the money to deliver on its promises.

This book outlines the mechanisms that transform the welfare state from a bright and benevolent entity into a dark, stingy and totalitarian government machine. The story of this transformation is highly relevant to an American audience. The mechanisms that turn bright into dark, that replaces well-meaning public policy with malicious fiscal fascism, are not unique to the Swedish welfare state. They are built into all welfare states.

It is only a matter of time before the transformation of the welfare state from bright to dark, from generous to stingy, takes place.

America is close behind Sweden. Five, maybe ten years at the most. But more important than predicting when we will see the dark side of the welfare state here, is the fact that it only takes one major law in Congress to bring the welfare state to its malicious, fiscally fascist turning point.

The bill for that law is already written, it is in committee and could be put before the House and the Senate any day.

Telling the story of what will happen once that bill is passed, and once America's welfare state is transformed, has not been an easy job for me. I grew up in Sweden believing, like everyone else there, that it was the best place in the world to be. I believed that the government should indeed provide for people from cradle to grave. I thought it was natural that our schools emphasized social justice and discouraged bright kids from excelling. I took for granted that only the government could provide people with health care. I assumed it was almost a law of nature that the government should pay people income security for being home from work.

It seemed entirely obvious to me that we should all try to fit in to the kind of lifestyle the government had in mind for us. And if we did not fit in, we bullied those who did not – called them outcasts, looked upon them as anomalies and problems. Those few among us who tried to say that more freedom, lower taxes and more individual choice would be good for us – well, they were branded by media, the government and the rest of us (all thinking alike) as something that is best called "unmutuals".

As I grew up, graduated high school and went to college, I saw the first signs of the transformation of the Swedish welfare state. Gradually it stopped providing for people and started defaulting on its promises. Budget cuts in health care, education, income security, elderly care and law enforcement gradually became the normal state of affairs. The services and entitlements that you would plan your life after – that you would take for granted because they were provided by the government – slowly withered away.

In the beginning it was all abstract and had no direct impact on my life. The seemingly marginal shift in focus from helping people to cutting that help away from the government's budget appeared at first to be part of an eclectic academic conversation with no real relevance to the rest of us. This is where America is today.

But time went by and budget cuts became permanent. And they spread to more and more areas of government. Slowly but steadily they began showing up in your everyday life.

I got married and became a parent. When my son was born we were asked to leave the hospital in just over 24 hours. After all, it was an uncomplicated delivery. (Today, at some government-run hospitals in Sweden mothers who have a no-complication delivery are asked to go home after six – *six* – hours.) Trying to be a foreseeing parent I looked at the schools my son would go to and noticed that as a result of budget cuts they had started hiring non-certified, lower-paid teachers in place of certified ones.

Occasionally, like all kids, my son needed health care. I noticed how the waiting lines had grown longer, how the co-pays in the socialized health system kept going up and how the medical staff had less time to care for their patients.

For the first year of my son's life I lived on Sweden's parental-leave income insurance system. As a parent you have the right to 12 months of income insurance benefits from the government to replace your regular income. When the program was created the replacement rate was 100 percent. Then it was cut to 90 percent. When I was on it, the pay was down to 80 percent.

Each time I had to interact with some government agency – and in Sweden you tend to do that a lot – I noticed how the bureaucrats' attitudes toward us citizens gradually changed for the worse. It was as though we were becoming a problem in their lives, something they wanted to have to deal with as little as possible.

Which, it turns out, was exactly what was going on. The more demands from citizens that government bureaucrats complied with – the more entitlement checks they wrote, the more patients they admitted to hospitals – the costlier the welfare state would be to the government.

And keeping costs down soon became the overarching priority for everything and anything the government did.

This was in the '90s. Everywhere I looked the welfare state was in retreat. Everywhere I turned, a politician told me there was no longer any money to pay for all their promises.

At the same time, taxes stayed high so there was no chance for me to provide for myself and my family without the defaulted-on promises from government.

To Americans, this all seems like an unreal situation. Since I moved to the United States in 2002 I have found it difficult to explain the deep, complex and destructive mechanisms that makes a welfare state turn on its own citizens.

With this book I hope to unravel the mystery of how and why a welfare state goes from being your good friend to your bad nightmare. In view of President Obama's solemn vow to "fundamentally remake" America I hope that my story, my analysis and my explanations of what has gone so wrong in Sweden can help America avoid the same disaster that Sweden is now rapidly becoming.

With that in mind I welcome you to the dark side of the welfare state.

# 1. THE DARK SIDE ON YOUR DOORSTEP

America's flirtation with the welfare state resembles the love affair in the 1981 supernatural cinematic thriller, "Ghost Story," wherein a young college professor meets a strange but beautiful woman, is mesmerized and embarks upon the love affair that defines his life and eventual death. The deeper he falls in love, the less attention he pays to his work. He becomes increasingly unproductive, neglects his duties and squanders his career, all because of the strange woman.

Not until it's too late does he realize that the object of his obsession has a very dark and sinister side. In the film's cosmology, she is the ghost of a woman whose death was caused long ago by the young man's father and his friends. By the time she delivers on her eerie promise –"and I will see the life run out of you" – he has nowhere to run.

As equally seductive, and equally destructive, as the preternatural woman are the promises made for our country's encroaching welfare state. At first glimpse, it appears as beneficent and fair, which are the love-at-first-sight qualities some Americans have developed, prompting their crush.

*The end of the beginning*

But a closer look also reveals a much darker side, a system of government that does not provide for its citizens, but treats them instead as problems, cost units – in effect, as enemies of the government budget. On the dark side, the welfare state maliciously turns on the people whom it is supposed to provide for, which it is forced to do to ensure the system's very survival.

Americans in general don't yet know the dark side of the welfare state. We are on the brink of it, but even with the passage of the "Obamacare" health reform bill the vicious, destructive side of big government barely has made itself known to the American people. One reason is that the health reform bill has not really gone into effect yet, but once it does it will be only a matter of time before we begin to see the dark side.

Furthermore, the health reform bill is far from the end of the statist ambition to grow our government. To paraphrase Winston Churchill: The healthcare bill is not the end of the expansion of government in America. It is not even the beginning of the end of that expansion. But it is the end of the beginning.

### Sweden's social and economic predicament

As big as government already is, it is only half the size it will be if such measures promoted by the current administration and Democrats in Congress are enacted. With the healthcare bill, Americans are now one step closer to Sweden. Other proposed reforms, if they become law, will leap us straight into the heartland of the destructive Scandinavian welfare state.

Your writer has lived under the dark side of the Scandinavian system, where I witnessed firsthand its devastating effects. In this book, I tell the story of that dark side, and how the government that was supposed to kindly and efficiently take care of its people gradually turned on its own citizens.

I explain how the welfare state can be turned into a business-class gulag where lives are shattered in the name of an ideology; where people have even committed suicide under the malicious pressure from a government they thought was supposed to lend them a helping hand.

I believe America needs to hear this story. On this side of the Atlantic, a considerable percentage of the population suffers from the perception that the welfare state is ultimately benevolent. These blinkered individuals anticipate only the bright side of a government that hands out money and provides services, seemingly for free.

The reality, however, is the exact opposite of the bright side. The dark side is harsh, stingy and, in its full-scale mode, malicious and downright mean. Where the bright side lends its citizens a helping hand, the dark side gives them a slap in the face. It ruins people's finances, their health and their lives.

The dark side of the welfare state transforms the citizen from an individual to a cost unit. Politicians and government bureaucrats no longer compete with each other to hand out more perks to people; they compete with each other to punish the people for being dependent on the government.

People die on the dark side of the welfare state. They die in government-run, tax-paid, budget-starved hospitals because the hospitals cannot afford enough doctors and nurses.

In Sweden, where the dark side has eclipsed a once thriving nation, 3,000 people die every year in the hands of a government-run, single-payer health system as a direct consequence of policies that the dark side brings about.[1] Ohio has about the same population as Sweden. If America adopted the Swedish health care model Ohio could therefore see 3,000 deaths every year at its hospitals as a result of hospitals being resource-starved, severely under-staffed and overburdened.

The dark side of the welfare state reaches well beyond health care. Middle-class families are forced to depend on government entitlements and put their financial security in the hands of politicians, yet when they ask for help they are denied benefits and hurled into financial ruin and poverty. Adding insult to injury, the middle class is taxed more heavily than the rich. The tipping point where benevolent becomes malevolent, where bright turns dark, is when the welfare state systematically and persistently starts reneging on its magnanimous promises. As Margaret Thatcher succinctly put it: "The only trouble with Socialism is that eventually you run out of other people's money."

America currently is reaching that tipping point beyond which there may be no return. Government encroachment into areas never imagined by the founding fathers add new entitlement programs that entrap the U.S. citizenry in dependencies hitherto unheard of here, but painfully well known to people in Europe, Swedes in particular. This entrapment follows a familiar pattern where the government first makes a promise to provide for its citizens; forces them to accept the promise through regulations and high taxes; and finally walks away from its promises because it does not have the money to deliver them.

The following chapters combine statistical analyses and real-life examples from actual people's lives to tell the story of what a malevolent welfare state inflicts on its people. The examples and analyses cover all essential areas of the welfare state: education, income security, the labor market and, of course, health care. They reveal what America will eventually become should our politicians keep adapting program after program from Swedish welfare models.

## The FIRST Act: government and income security

Three decades after completing its welfare state, Sweden is today a society on the verge of social and economic collapse. From the world's highest taxes[2] to crime rates that are two, three, even up to six times higher than in other European countries,[3] Sweden is no longer the land of milk and honey that it was portrayed as when its welfare state gained international reputation. Today, the milk has gone sour and the honey is stale. A majority of the people depends on the government just to make ends meet every month and their standard of living has barely increased in almost 30 years. Sweden has plunged from being one of the most prosperous nations in the world in the early 1970s to something that I will later define as industrial poverty. If the United States doesn't heed the empirical lessons of the Swedish welfare experiment, it will succumb to the same failures.

As an example of what the dark side does to people, let me introduce you to Sofie K., a normal 24-year-old Swedish woman. In 2007 she and her husband had a baby boy. They named him Viktor. Sadly, seven months into his life, Viktor developed cancer. Eight months later, the child died.

His parents were, of course, devastated by their loss. Sofie, who was not working at that time, applied for assistance from the government's income security system. Taking for granted that the death of their son would be reason enough for Sofie to receive the income compensation, the young parents concentrated on their grief.

Little did they know that the death of their son was only the first act of a tragedy that would devastate their lives. Little did they know what the government had in mind for.

But before we learn more about Viktor's parents, let us take a look at a bill that the U.S. Congress is considering. This bill, known as the Family Income to Respond to Significant Transitions Act, or the FIRST Act, or HR 2339, was introduced in the U.S. House of Representatives by Congresswoman Lynn Woolsey (D-Calif.) in May 2009.[4] It suggests the introduction of a Swedish-style income security system for all Americans, the same kind that Viktor's parents back in Sweden relied on.

It is comprehensive enough, and adds enough taxes and government spending to the U.S. economy, to push us over the breaking point in to the territory of the dark side of the welfare state.

FIRST has 24 cosponsors[5] and has been in the Education and Labor Committee since October of 2009. Although many people have probably never heard of it, it may very well be the next item on Congress' agenda now that the health care reform has passed.

The FIRST bill suggests that Congress:

establish a program that supports the efforts of States to provide partial or full wage replacement to new parents, so that the new parents are able to spend time with a new infant or newly adopted child, and to other employees, and for other purposes.

In other words, if you have a baby, get sick or cannot go to work for any reason that the federal government approves of, your state government will send you a check to replace your lost income. This is called *general income security*, which is widespread in Europe but not yet here in America.

A reader may ask, "What is the harm in that? After all, such programs already exist for government workers. There is the Family Medical Leave Act for federal employees."

To begin with, the FIRST act would go much farther than FMLA. It would provide more benefits and would cover the entire American workforce, far beyond what workers compensation covers.

Workers compensation is strictly for wage losses as a result of workplace injuries. The FIRST Act would pay every American to stay home from work for a host of reasons that have nothing to do with disability or old age. Primarily the act's purpose is to provide income security under temporary sick leave. The FIRST Act also allows for an endless range of new eligibilities in the future. The commitment from the federal government is open-ended.

Back now to Viktor's parents. At the time of her son's death, Sofie was on a sick-leave program with the Swedish income security agency. It was her wish to remain on sick leave after her son died, assuming that her benefits would continue uninterrupted while she grieved the loss of her son.

A couple of days after Viktor's death, Sofie called the local office of the national income insurance agency to confirm her extended benefits. She was then told that her benefits had been terminated on the day of her son's death.

Why?

This is where the welfare state reveals its dark side.

The government had promised to cover her income losses when she is unable to work. It gave her the right to be on sick leave or any other leave that pertains to urgent family needs. No doubt, the need to grieve and take care of the funeral of one's child is an urgent one, or so thought Sofie and the therapist at the hospital who helped her through the first couple of days after Viktor's death.

But the government denied her application for sick-leave benefits, because she had not been available to look for a job neither the day of nor the day after her son's death. The income security agency specifically demanded that the instant her son was dead she should go out and look for a job. Until she did, she would be denied compensation from the income security agency.[6]

There is a sinister reason behind the requirement on Sofie to go out and look for a job. The income security system in Sweden stopped working. It does not have the cash it needs to pay for all the benefits the government has promised people. Too many people are cashing in their entitlements and too few are working to pay the taxes that sustain the income security system.

*Not quite what was promised*

Sofie K. is but one victim of a systemic flaw inherent within any income security system.

These systems are funded by taxes. The Swedish government runs its income security through a payroll tax. (It is unclear how the income security systems in the FIRST act would be funded.) The more benefits the government promises, the more they raise taxes to pay for them. The more benefits they promise, the longer people stay away from work. An example: Swedes take twice as many sick days as Americans do every year.[7]

When people stay home from work, less work gets done. When employers pay higher payroll taxes, common sense and basic arithmetic dictate that under the same revenues they have less money left for hiring employees. As a result, fewer people are employed and less work gets done. When combined, increased absence due to the benefits and lower employment due to the taxes result in lower tax revenues for the income security system than politicians anticipated when it was inaugurated.

Additionally, Swedes pay the highest taxes in the world. They pay 30 percent to 33 percent in local income taxes, depending on the city and county where they live. On top of that, many of them pay another 20 percent to 25 percent in national income taxes. Payroll taxes are 32 percent, or twice as high as in the United States. Swedes also pay value added tax on private consumption: everything from their apartment lease and utility bills to train tickets, clothes, furniture and food is taxed at a rate anywhere between 12 and 25 percent.

Needless to say they are much poorer than U.S. citizens – provided, of course, that bills resembling the FIRST Act do not become law. Swedish families cannot set money aside for contingencies like family tragedies, let alone for more regular occasions of income losses such as sickness or job transitions.

Swedes must accept the fact that they give away large chunks of their income to the government and then hope that the government will give it back to them when they need it. The problem is that the Swedish government has promised away more money than it takes in – and it takes in insufficient revenues precisely because of all the promises it must fulfill.

Sweden cannot raise taxes any more than it already has. It is simply not possible. The only way they can keep the general income security system going is by trying to cut expenses – to simply provide significantly less in services than what Sweden's citizenry pays for with their taxes.

From this writer's experience, it is not unreasonable to predict that the same thing will happen here in America should the FIRST Act or something similar actually pass. As a result we will have countless cases like that of Viktor's mom.

*When revenues do not match spending*

Let us hypothetically say that the U.S. Government sets up a FIRST Act-style general income security system. Congress will obviously have to provide some sort of budget for the program; let us say they expect to pay out $100 in income security payments per year. Suppose also that they design a payroll tax that will bring in $100 to pay for it.

The problem for the government is that it cannot tell people, "We will pay out $100 and not a dime more" in income security. If they did then obviously the program would not be what it claims to be – a general income security plan for every American. It would be a first-come-first-served, limited-supplies-only program forcing people to rush in order to collect their benefits. Even if the government estimates that they will not have to spend more than $100 per year in the income security program, they cannot stop spending from going up when people file more claims.

Because the benefits are so attractive and easily attained, people take more sick days off from work. Less work is performed, resulting in less production and personal income and, finally, lower payroll tax revenues funding the government's general income security program.

When tax revenues fall to, say, $90 and costs go up to, say, $110, the government is stuck between a rock and a hard place: either it has to rein in uncontrollable spending or it has to raise taxes. If we have already reached the high point of what taxpayers are going to put up with, the only alternative that remains for the government is to cut benefits.

Politicians will not do away with the income security system per se (when was the last time our government terminated an entitlement program?). Instead they will start to twist and tweak technical aspects of the program. One such tweak is to tighten the rules for when, how and why people can claim their income insurance benefits.

Such a change of rules occurs long after people adjusted their lives to high taxes and government income insurance programs: they have no financial margins to build any income security of their own.

They end up in the same situation as Viktor's parents.

They adjusted their family's finances to the Swedish income security system – and to the country's confiscatory taxes. But the government changed the rules of the game. The general income security agency has ramped up its denials of benefit claims: it now requires that many people on sick leave go look for a job, which is motivated by the agency's urgent need to cut costs.

More people are home on benefits instead of working and paying income taxes. As a result, government tax revenues are down – in our hypothetical example, let us say to $90 instead of the $100 that the politicians expected when they created the program. Since the government is spending $110 it has a budget balancing problem. As we said above, once government can no longer raise taxes its only opportunity is to limit access to benefits.

If the income insurance agency denies one in eleven claims the total payouts will fall to $100. These denials will not be based on examinations of the claimant's actual case, but *entirely on the government's need to cut its spending*. Since it is perfectly possible that each and every one of these denied claims are legitimate by the eligibility rules that the income insurance program was founded on, the government now has to invent new rules that have nothing to do with people's actual eligibility. Or, the government can simply hire its own doctor that examines applications for sick leave income compensation with only one goal in mind: to deny the claim. This is the route Sweden's income insurance agency has taken.

As for the people, they are made worse off in two steps. First, they have to pay higher taxes and as a result have less money left over to build their own financial security buffer. Secondly, once they need the income security that the government has promised (as will happen if the FIRST Act becomes law here in the United States) they are denied those benefits.

This is how the welfare state turns dark. When it was still on its bright side, the Swedish welfare state treated Sofie K. as a citizen who could count on the government for her care. But once the government realized that it was in over its head because it did not have all the money it needed for its entitlement system, it depersonalized Sofie K. and countless other people.

It started treating them as budget items. Cost units.

Once the government's entitlement system is overloaded and strapped on cash (the inevitable outcome of such entitlement systems as income security programs) the bureaucracy that runs it will shift its focus from helping people to fixing the government's underfunded mistake. When the program is new, its first priority is to help people. When it is established and runs short on cash, its priorities shift. The bureaucracy created to administer the program subsequently shifts its efforts to helping the government balance its budget.

Since at this point the government cannot raise taxes, it needs to cut costs. The only way to do this is to deny people some or all of the money to which they are entitled. The only way the politicians and bureaucrats can do this is by transforming people from individuals with needs to depersonalized cost units. It is easier for bureaucrats to deny people money that they would have previously received if people are no longer people but items on a spreadsheet.

*Down the slope of statism*

Once the income security system comes to this point of relegating its citizens to cost-unit status, why don't people simply vote for politicians that will dismantle it? Is the dark side of the welfare state inevitable?

The immediate response to this question is another question: does anyone know of a single tax-paid entitlement program jettisoned by politicians? It speaks volumes that we can all name numerous entitlement programs off the top of our heads that the government has created, but not one that the government has terminated. As Ronald Reagan said:

"No government ever voluntarily reduces itself in size. Government programs, once launched, never disappear. Actually, a government bureau is the nearest thing to eternal life we'll ever see on this earth."

Reagan's adage definitely holds true in Sweden. Even the Conservative Party, a.k.a., The Moderates, fully embraces the redistributive welfare state. However, conservatives in America do not have much of a better track record.[8] With the exception of President Reagan, no leading conservative in post-Franklin Roosevelt America has made any concerted effort to dismantle the federal government's big entitlement programs. Not even the much-touted "end to welfare" reform under the 1990s Republican Congressional majority ended any welfare programs. The reform merely shifted the operational responsibility from the federal government to the states; the federal government still pays for those programs.[9]

The deeper explanation to why government is a perpetual machine lies partly in the fact that once in the welfare state is in place, politicians tend to adapt to it. Every new generation of politicians accepts the current state of affairs, gradually drawing the conclusion that currently existing entitlement programs, taxes and levels of government spending are natural parts of the political environment.

They also tend to fear that threatening the entitlement programs would upset voters who, in turn, might retaliate at the ballot box. The bigger the welfare state gets, the bigger the politicians' fear grows. Succumbing to the slow boil of the welfare state, exacerbated by politicians' fears of losing elections, virtually guarantees that nothing will be done to stem the mounting problems of out-of-control entitlement spending and onerous taxes.

But there is a third factor in all this, a more profound driving force that makes it even harder for most politicians to break with their habit of taking the welfare state for granted: ideology.

*The welfare state: a start with no end*

As absurd as it may seem, liberals and conservatives are not all that different when it comes to big government. Their ideological foundations may look very different, but both liberalism and conservatism promote big government. They do it in different ways, but the end result is similar: bigger, more intrusive government paid for with higher, more burdensome taxes.

Here is how it works. There are mainly two reasons to expand government: to redistribute income and to instill compassion and other virtues. Neither liberals nor conservatives can lay claim to the high ground in either instance.

In fact, conservatives started growing government long before their liberal counterparts. Driven by compassion and the will to define a social morality, they brought government into the business of educating children. In his book "Feds in the Classroom: How Big Government Corrupts, Cripples and Compromises American Education," Neal McCluskey explains how government entered into the lives of our children:

> Of course, children did not just wake up one day to find truancy officers at their doors demanding that they get an education or to discover that their little red schoolhouses had been transformed into massive, impersonal industrial edifices. No, government domination came gradually. Indeed, the process began as far back as the colonial era, and even [President] Jefferson himself, who believed that an educated citizenry is essential for a democracy's survival, had a hand in it.[10]

McCluskey traces the first step toward public education back to the Commonwealth of Massachusetts in 1642, with a law that mandated "that households provide education to their children, lest the young be removed and 'put forth as apprentices.'"

The reason behind this strong mandate was entirely one of virtuous citizenship – the desire by conservatives to create one common morality for society. McCluskey quotes from The Old Deluder Satan Act, enacted in Massachusetts in 1647,[11] which was a law that threatened parents with removal of their kids unless they got them an education:

> It being the chief project of the old deluder, Satan, to keep men from the knowledge of the scriptures, it is therefore ordered that every township in this jurisdiction, after the Lord hath increased them to fifty households shall forthwith appoint one within their town to teach all such children as shall resort to him to write and read.[12]

By 1830 government was so deeply involved in education that permanent school bureaucracies had emerged. The "common schools" were a brainchild of this same paternalistic philosophy. Its proponents felt that:

> only a centralized [school] system, run by experts ... could transcend the parochialism of local schools and districts controlled by people of similar religious, ethnic, and social background, and socialize children so that they would become what their betters considered 'good Americans.'[13]

This expansion of government was not the work of liberals. It was not driven by the socialist rationales for bigger government, and redistribution of income and wealth. On the contrary, it was driven by a desire to preserve the norms and ethical standards of their time. But the establishing of school bureaucracies was nevertheless an infringement on individual freedom. Under full educational freedom, every school has its own set of norms and values with the aim that students adopt those norms and values. With a monopoly on children's education, the government inevitably creates a norms-and-values monopoly. Government defines what it means to be virtuous.

As minuscule as this may seem, it is nevertheless the first government step toward the modern welfare state. By taking monopoly on education the government moves outside its core responsibilities, namely the protection of life, liberty and property. As history tells us, there is no end to government's involvement in our lives once it steps outside of those core responsibilities.

But what is so bad about a common set of norms? A good question, indeed. Every society needs a basic moral platform to build on. But beyond protecting our rights to life, liberty and the pursuit of happiness, the government has no right to impose any other moral values and norms. This is nevertheless what conservatives have done through the centuries, with the explicit purpose to raise "good citizens" that will preserve the existing society. The good citizen, in their worldview, does not challenge the existing social order but strives to protect it and perpetuate it.

Essentially, conservatives socialized education, traditionally considered a civic albeit private responsibility. It is responsible to raise one's children to the best of one's ability, including providing them with a good education. But when conservatives expanded government's role in education, their agenda reached beyond seizing control of public education into curriculum content determined by government bureaucrats.

Government socialized a civic virtue and to some extent reduced the function of parents from providing nurturing and moral guidance of their children to simple biological units that provide nothing more than food, clothing and shelter to newly created wards of the state.

This transfer of responsibilities from citizens to the government is the very nature of the welfare state. Especially during the 1800s the welfare state got put on tracks, both in terms of practical policy and in terms of redistributive ideology, to the intrusive size it has now assumed. The growth from the first steps toward socializing education to the 21st century and "Obamacare" has two motivators – conservative compassion and liberal redistribution – but it follows one straight trajectory.

As a matter of fact, in addition to education health care has been one field where conservatives have expanded government's oversight in order to impose norms and values upon the country's populace. Unlike current ambitions to nationalize the entire health care system, past conservative efforts were limited to health care for the poor.

Tax-funded government hospitals existed in North America since at least the 1700s.[14] Conservatives created them because they thought it virtuous to take care of the poor. No rational person can find fault with looking out for the medical needs of the disadvantaged, but relying on government to do it makes no sense to this writer whatsoever.

Nevertheless, this is exactly what happened. From the beginning of the 18th century, state governments built public hospitals, and even created government-run health insurance systems. The first occurrence of a government-operated insurance program was in 1798.[15]

By the early 20th century, the federal government regulated the markets for vaccines, sera and other medicines as well as food. This is yet another example of a conservative virtue converted into a government bureaucracy. Such programs undermined the responsibility of private citizens over what they produced, sold, bought and used.

There is no doubt that a more complex world makes it more complex to be a consumer. Health care today is a much more complicated matter today than it was in the 19th century – though of course also much more efficient and accurate. But these new complexities don't warrant further government incursions into our private lives. Our means of transportation have also grown far more complex, and yet outside the Obama administration very few people think it is a good idea that the government owns a car manufacturer. Most of us are perfectly capable of taking care of ourselves, seeing to our own needs, doing business with other private citizens and assuming responsibility for our own lives. In fact, for some, that is precisely what it means to be free.

Yet conservatives have helped create a government that holds people's hands and protects them from all kinds of decisions that adults are perfectly capable of making. While the world has gotten more complex, individuals have grown more sophisticated as members of society and therefore better equipped to make choices that might impact their lives.

*Growing government: liberals and conservatives join forces*

Liberals began expanding government much later than conservatives. Their basic motivation is income redistribution, a political idea hatched in the latter half of the 19th century.[16] It gained ground in Europe at that time but did not really gain a foothold in America until the Franklin D Roosevelt administration.

One of the most obvious expressions of FDR-era radical liberalism was the rapid and reckless increase in federal income taxes. While income taxes alone do not redistribute income, they do so indirectly if higher incomes are taxed more heavily than lower incomes, which forces high-income earners to contribute a disproportionate share to government spending. Most government spending programs benefit low-income families. The combination of such programs and high marginal income tax rates means that the government is deeply complicit in income redistribution.

On President Roosevelt's watch, personal income taxes rose dramatically.[17] The lowest tax rate in 1931 was 1 percent and the highest tax rate was 20 percent. In 1936, after one term of FDR in the White House and a Democrat majority in Congress, the lowest income tax rate was 4 percent. The highest rate had climbed to a confiscatory 75 percent.

On top of the tax hikes, Roosevelt lowered the income threshold for federal taxes from $10,000 in 1931 to $4,000 in 1936.

The FDR administration also went after businesses. The corporate income tax was 11 percent in 1929 and 13.5 percent by 1934. Over the next four years the Democrats took away the income tax exemption for corporations and introduced an increasingly complicated system of marginal tax rates on corporate income. By 1938, businesses started paying 12.5 percent in taxes and as much as 19 percent in the top income bracket.

In other words, the FDR years were not exactly modest when it came to confiscatory taxation. But his immodesty did not stop there: between 1932 and 1939 federal non-defense spending increased by 400 percent. By comparison, GDP increased by a relatively modest 57 percent. When World War II started, federal spending was still very small by today's standards. Nevertheless, the legacy of the FDR administration is one of aggressive government expansion. Progressive taxes combined with government spending directed at low-income Americans institutionalized redistribution of income between America's wealthy and poor.[18]

Democrats have stuck to the redistribution agenda. They have grown government in practically every conceivable part of our economy and our lives. And at some point, it was inevitable that their quest for ever bigger government would coincide with the conservative quest to socialize more and more of our civic responsibilities. It was inevitable that at some point liberals would come up with a government spending program that conservatives could affix their signature as if it were their own: Medicaid.

Medicaid is a milestone in the rise of the American welfare state. This comprehensive health insurance program possesses a distinctly compassionate element – it was created for the poor – and when combined with steep federal marginal income taxes, the rich pay for health care for the poor. It therefore satisfies both conservative and liberal rationales to expand government.

Cross-party line agreement on Medicaid and Medicare may not have started with the creation of the program. When they became law in 1965 an overwhelmingly Democrat majority in Congress voted for them.[19] However, since then four out of five Republican presidents have signed laws to expand either Medicaid or Medicare, or both. Through both programs, and Medicaid in particular, the conservative desire to socialize virtue and compassion has fused with the liberal desire to redistribute income.

Not even the conservative icon, President Reagan, escapes criticism on this issue. He approved incremental steps in Medicaid coverage for children. He also took Medicaid beyond the realms of legal citizenry. By 1985 Medicaid eligibility requirements largely matched the requirements for the Aid to Families with Dependent Children program and therefore effectively qualified as a modest expression for conservative compassion. But in 1986 Reagan signed a bill that made it mandatory for states to open Medicaid to illegal immigrants who "otherwise would be eligible", i.e., would qualify if they were in the country legally.[20]

Again in 1987 Reagan let Medicaid grow beyond the realms of a poverty relief program. Congress passed, and he signed into law, a general income eligibility increase for pregnant women up to 185 percent of the poverty limit.

While expansion of Medicaid often comes at the initiative of redistributionist liberals, conservatives are willing to go along because they want to appear as compassionate. Since previous generations of conservative politicians have expanded Medicaid, new generations of conservative politicians pile their show of compassion on top of the compassion that others have already signed into law.

Liberals, of course, love this. They get to redistribute more and more money, and as they tie conservatives to the bills that expand government, the job becomes increasingly difficult for others – like those pesky small-government advocates – who want to turn back the tidal wave of ever-growing government.

As if to reinforce this joint purpose of conservative compassion and liberal redistribution to grow government, the 1997 Republican-controlled Congress passed a bill to create SCHIP (also known as "Medicaid for Kids"). At the time the program was trumpeted as a poverty relief program, which would make it pass the conservative compassionate litmus test.

Initially, SCHIP did come across as strictly poverty relief. In 1997, 14.5 million children lived in poverty in the United States. That same year, SCHIP enrolled 14.7 million children. Almost a perfect match, at least statistically.

Ten years later, in 2007, both Congress and the White House had been in Republican hands for most of SCHIP's existence. By that time the number of poor kids had dropped to 13 million. Yet SCHIP enrollment had grown by almost 50 percent from 1997 levels to 21 million children. Compassionate conservative Republicans ensured during its first decade of operation that SCHIP expanded enrollment from 20 percent of all children in America to 28 percent.

Modern-day compassionate conservatives follow in the footsteps of their 18th and 19th century ideological forefathers. Together with redistribution-addicted liberals they have created the perfect storm of ever-growing government. Evidence is plentiful. During the George W Bush administration, Congress created or expanded funding for a host of entitlement programs, including:

- The Medicare prescription plan
- Title 1 education funds for low-income families
- No Child Left Behind
- Temporary Assistance to Needy Families
- Women, Infants and Children (WIC), and special supplemental food program
- Food Stamp Program
- Public housing programs
- Head Start

All of these programs represent some form of income redistribution, are permanent and, for the most part, dole out money or open in-kind programs for people who clearly make more than the federal poverty limit.

The umbrella name for Medicaid, SCHIP and all the welfare state programs listed above is "Federal Aid to States." In a joint effort by compassionate conservatives and liberal redistributionists, Congress increased Federal Aid to States between 1998 and 2007 by a whopping 74 percent.[21]

Before the President Obama administration's stimulus package, Federal Aid to States was closing in on $500 billion annually. With the American Recovery Reinvestment Act included, the final tally exceeds $1 trillion.

What makes SCHIP and all the Federal Aid to States programs such a blend between conservative compassion and liberal redistribution is the fact that they target low-income families and are paid for predominantly by the federal government. The federal government, in turn, gets the bulk of its money from income taxes[22] (at least that is how it used to be before President Obama started borrowing to make federal payroll). Federal income taxes are paid for by high-income earners: 70 percent of federal income taxes come from the top ten percent income earners.[23]

Conservative compassion fused with liberal redistribution is a troubling recipe for a never-ending growth of government.

Which brings us back to the FIRST Act.

*You – an irritating cost unit*

Despite the fact that our government is big, and despite the fact that the Internal Revenue Service is the largest tax collection agency in the world, we are still not as far down the big government road as Europe. Our government has thus far stayed focused on spending money to satisfy our needs: education; highways; poverty relief in the form of public housing and food stamps; and health insurance for low-income families. This has definitely grown our government, but as incredible as it may seem, there are still large areas of our lives where, if we lived in Sweden, we would have to put up with even more government. A lot more, in fact.

The FIRST Act will cover one of those last spots. It will open a can of government expansion worms so big that the differences between America and the Europe I left will wither away.

So far Americans have lived by the principle that we all build our own economic security for events such as illness, the birth of a child or if we need to care for someone in our family. It is part of what makes us free and independent. That room for self determination – among the last remaining ones in our country – will vanish with the FIRST Act.

I cannot overstate the consequences that this will have.

A fundamental principle of American freedom is that we determine the course of our own lives with others as we choose. The principle of self determination is not just words on paper – it means something real to us. It means that we are free to build and live our lives and pursue happiness independently and together with others as we choose. It means that instead of relying on the government, we create and pursue opportunities for ourselves.

Ours is a society of opportunity.

By contrast, unlike the United States, European nations in general and Sweden in particular, are old kingdoms built and sustained by the rulers, not the people. Compared to the American tradition of self determination and self reliance, European populations have a long tradition of government reliance. Before parliamentary democracy, the government – the monarch – told them what they could and could not do. Benevolent kings provided for their peoples, or punished them fiercely when they opposed him.

Dependency on government is a historically codified aspect of Europe's history. For this reason it was easy to build welfare states there: generations had grown up expecting government to provide for them and tell them what they could and could not do. It turned out to be a smooth transition from a king to a paternalistic welfare state.

This cultural difference between Americans and Europeans marks the difference between a society built on the concept of individual freedom and a society built on the tradition of government authority. The more of the European welfare state we bring here, the more we blur those distinctions.

Under a European-style big government, American prosperity will wither away. The fundamental culture of our society will change from entrepreneurship and opportunity to statism and dependency.

It is not possible to unite the welfare state with the principles upon which the United States was built. By definition the welfare state creates dependency on government. Government powers are no longer enumerated, as prescribed by our Constitution.

At the heart of the transition from an opportunity society to a welfare state lies the fact that the government no longer exists for you. You exist for the government.

You are no longer a citizen. You are a cost unit in cash-strapped entitlement programs, a work unit as a taxpayer and the government's own self-replenishing tax ATM.

You are on the dark side of the welfare state.

Few people know the bitter taste of what this means in reality like Mr. Johan S., a 53-year-old Swedish farm worker.[24] He has been working for almost four decades. He proudly earned his own money, took care of himself all his life and avoided becoming dependent on someone else, including the government.

A couple of years ago he had an accident and badly injured his knee. To make matters worse he injured the knee again during the healing process, leaving him with a recurring pain problem.

The streak of bad luck continued when he was diagnosed with leukemia in spring 2009.

This is the type of person big government proponents refer to when they advocate for more government. Therefore, when the government is unable to honor its commitments to those who find themselves in such an obviously bad situation, it should serve as a huge warning to any country seeking to replicate similar programs.

The leukemia medications prescribed Johan could not be taken with the painkillers for his knee, making it impossible for him to work. As a result, he filed a request for income security payments with Sweden's Income Insurance Agency in much the same way an American worker would under the FIRST Act.

The Income Insurance Agency is set up specifically to provide income supplements for people who, like Johan, are unable to work. The agency's programs are funded by a 32 percent payroll tax (more than twice the payroll taxes American employers pay for their employees).

Everything should be fine, right? Before we get there, let us read Johan's description of his condition:

> I was back at work the Monday after Midsummer and the rest of the summer I worked maybe every other day. Luckily I have a very good employer who let me go home on the days when it just does not work for me, when the pain has been too much and I am consumed by tiredness. But when I started taking medicine against the leukemia last fall nothing worked for me anymore, I could maybe put in five minutes at a time. See, one of the side effects is that I cannot take any painkillers for the knee.[25]

So did the Income Insurance Agency send him a check? Not exactly:

> The National Income Insurance Agency explains that he can forget being on sick leave.... On November 11 his application was denied, since he is considered sufficiently able to work.[26]

Now – wait a minute. What is going on here? The Income Insurance Agency is a bureaucracy, but aren't they supposed to write checks?

That is what the proponents of the FIRST Act would have us believe. When American liberals say they want general income security for all, they do not tell us about the flip side of the coin.

In order to make sure that people actually qualify for sick leave income security, the Swedish Income Insurance Agency has employed its own physicians who make an independent valuation of the documentation that comes with each claim. These physicians, in turn, supposedly perform strictly professional evaluations based solely on their own medical expertise.

However, as it has become more and more difficult for government to generate enough tax revenues to pay for its entitlement programs, the Income Insurance Agency charged its physicians with a somewhat different task: Rather than evaluating applications based strictly on medical factors, the physicians now evaluate applications based on what is called "budgetary medicine."

When the government cannot afford all the claims that people file the Income Insurance Agency is ordered to slash its budget *without formally retreating from the entitlements* that the government has handed out to people.

The disastrous result is that regular citizens are trapped in a welfare state that no longer places their needs highest on its agenda. On the contrary, they are now victims of entitlement systems that do their best *not to give them* what they have been assured is their entitlement.

At this point, citizens are transformed into little more than irritating cost units. Johan is far from the only cancer patient who learned this lesson the hard way. Reports *Dagens Nyheter*, one of Sweden's largest newspapers:

> Specialist physicians concerned: While waiting to die, chronically ill cancer patients are forced out on the job market. 'We do not think it is reasonable that very ill cancer patients – with a bad outlook – should be forced to work despite the fact that they suffer from difficult symptoms such as pain, tiredness, psychological repercussions [from the disease] side effects of their treatment. [27]

A welfare state in decline, spearheaded by a cash-strapped income insurance system is easy to identify: The politicians who run it begin introducing new concepts as well as change eligibility rules to keep people from getting entitlements. Cynically speaking, a masterful example of this kind of budget-driven creativity is the "discovery" of "residual labor capacity" among terminally ill cancer patients such as Johan S.

The original concept was an income insurance system that benefited people, but it evolved into a program featuring bureaucrats and legislators scrambling desperately for ways to deny people the money they were promised. The resulting panic prompts public servants to implement desperate measures such as the Swedish bureaucrats who force terminally ill cancer patients to work.

As unbelievably cruel and heartless as this is, it is nevertheless a real-world example of how politicians and bureaucrats respond when their own good-hearted entitlement systems no longer work. Under normal circumstances, no sane person would require terminally ill cancer patients to work. But the dark side of the welfare state is not a state of normal circumstances. Rather, it is a perversion of the good intentions of political ideologues eager to defend the welfare state beyond common sense and any concern for human dignity and decency.

But still – how can this transformation take place without any significant or even noticeable opposition? How come people are not out in the streets protesting? And how can the bureaucracies that run these entitlement systems simply adapt from helping people to hindering them?

Important questions, indeed. In our pursuit of answers, let us meet yet another victim of the dark side of the welfare state, a 61-year-old woman with serious health problems:

> For many years Mari-Louise had suffered from serious health problems, physical as well as psychological, but several times tried to start working again. A few years ago

she moved from Stockholm to Dalarna to get closer to her daughter and her grandchildren. ... At the Income Insurance Agency's local office in [the city of] Borlange they were conducting an investigation into the possibility that Mari-Louise would be put on a permanent income benefit due to her health problems.[28]

Her doctor considered her medical problems to be so overwhelming that he deemed her unable to work, period. But the Income Insurance Agency thought differently. Without ever talking to her personal doctor...

...a case manager [at the Income Insurance Agency] wrote a letter to Mari-Louise declaring that her request for sick-leave related income insurance was denied. Instead she was told that she was now available to the labor market again.[29]

Even in good times, jobs for a 61-year-old woman are about as common in Sweden as touchdowns are in Yankee Stadium. This occurred in the midst of 2009's hard-hitting economic crisis.

So here we have a woman who has fought multiple health problems for many years, both physical and psychological. She packed up and moved to be closer to her family and bring some peace and stability to her life. She attempted repeatedly to return to her old job, but ultimately failed due to her health problems. She has done her very best to comply with whatever the welfare state in general, and its income security system in particular, requires of her.

Against this background, perhaps her reaction to the Income Insurance Agency's claim denial was understandable:

When the letter from the Income Insurance Agency arrived on Thursday before Easter it made Mari-Louise very upset. She cancelled all her plans for the Easter holiday, called her children in complete devastation. She was found dead on

Easter Sunday in a pile of documents like medical opinions from her physician and letters from government agencies. There was no suicide letter, only a piece of paper with the word "Sorry."[30]

So why is there no public outrage in Sweden? How come there is no massive political movement to put an end to this terrible abuse of government power?

The answers to these questions bear a chilling echo of President Reagan's ominous warnings that freedom is never more than one generation away from extinction. Today's Swedish politicians, just like practically every native-born Swede alive today, are children of the socialist welfare state. They have been socialized into a society where everyone takes for granted that the government takes care of you. Alternatives to government are more or less unthinkable. Therefore, when the government fails there is no genuine gut instinct that kicks in and tells the average Swede to seek alternatives. Politicians react the same way.

Popular protests are more common in European countries other than Sweden, but their politicians are just as determined to preserve the welfare state to which they have all grown accustomed. One major reason for this is that protests, rallies and riots in countries with big welfare states – such as in Greece recently – are not against a big, abusive government, but *in defense of* that same big government.

This stands in stark contrast to America where the Tea Party movements rally against government, not in its defense.

However, if the Obama administration and a liberal Congress succeed – if they get to "fundamentally remake" America as Obama vowed to do when he ran for president; and if "Obamacare" stands and the FIRST Act becomes law – then today's Tea Party movement may be the last widespread voice of freedom in America.

It only took one generation to transform Europe into a massive welfare state. It will not take more than one generation for a similar transformation in America. President Reagan's words about the fragility of freedom are as true today as they have ever been.

## The subtle transition

The transition from the bright side of the welfare state where people are treated as individuals in need of help to the dark side where they are treated as irritating cost units is a sneaky process that starts with small, seemingly insignificant changes to the daily work at government bureaucracies. Lets us use the so far non-existent Income Insurance Agency as an example. Someone quits and the position is not filled. Instead the workload is spread among the others – a marginal, barely noticeable change the first time it happens.

Slowly, government agencies receive new directives from higher in the hierarchy, directives that do not change the fundamental eligibility principles, but prescribe a somewhat more "careful" or "meticulous" approach to people's claims for income security benefits. Some directives urge the employees to employ extra-strict requirements for all documentation submitted by applicants. If a person wants wage replacement for sick leave, the officers of the Income Insurance Agency verify the claim by actually calling the applicant's physician and employer.

Over time the new directives get stricter and the workload heavier. Fewer and fewer retirees at the agency are replaced. People who apply for sick leave have to submit more and more documents and sign more and more affidavits. Due to the increased workload it takes longer and longer for the agency to process applications. This is deliberate, of course.

At some point the government starts changing the formal eligibility requirements. Think of it as raising the retirement age in Social Security, or putting a new income cap that would disqualify many people from enrolling. They have been planning all their lives to rely on Social Security, and suddenly they are locked out of it. Changes to general income security programs work the same way: working families plan their finances based on what the eligibility criteria are for those programs, and are left out in the cold when those criteria are changed.

When this has happened in Sweden, the employees of the Income Insurance Agency who meet with the applicants have to carry the heavy workload for the government. They have to explain eye-to-eye why a claim that would have been approved a month ago is suddenly denied. Customer relations that were smooth and friendly only recently soon turn more and more negative. And the staff reductions continue.

If the job market is still good, more and more people leave the Income Insurance Agency for less stressful jobs. But when the government has grown to such proportions that it is providing income security for all Americans, the burden on the economy will have slowed down economic growth, increasing unemployment to such levels that it is very difficult to find a new job, especially for those who quit a well-paid, benefits-loaded government job.

This is exactly what has happened in Sweden. As we will see later, the Swedish economy has found it increasingly difficult to produce enough jobs for its workforce for as long as 40 years now. The taxes that, absurdly enough, pay for the income security programs are themselves a source of discouragement to many employers. Being forced to pay a 32 percent tax on top of payroll is enough to keep businesses from hiring more people.

All the other taxes that are supposed to fund the welfare state add to the burden on the private sector. A 12-percent health care tax is part of an income tax that for the highest earners claim 57 percent on the margin. Up to 25 percent in value added tax weigh down consumer spending. Added together, these taxes are supposed to pay for the gargantuan Swedish welfare state.

American taxpayers will face similar taxes once the welfare state is fully grown here.

The bigger the welfare state, the more people will be dependent on it. Some estimates suggest that Sweden's unemployment rate over the past 15 years has remained consistently between 15 and 20 percent.[31] The more people who live off the welfare state, the fewer people will be paying taxes to support it. As fewer people pay taxes, the welfare state suffers mounting revenue problems; as its revenue problems grow, the welfare state gradually turns its dark side on people.

Even the bureaucrats get trapped on the dark side. If they comply with their bosses and do everything they can to deny people their claims, they will obviously have a workday filled with conflicts, hostility and overall negative confrontations with people. If, on the other, they quit their job it's possible they may never find a new one. So they put up with an increasingly unbearable workload, persistent conflicts with clients and the perpetual pressure from their bosses to deny more claims that the government cannot afford.

When people are forced to live with a stronger loyalty to government than to their fellow citizens, things have gotten pretty bad.

## 2. CRADLE TO GRAVE: FASTER WITH SOCIALIZED HEALTH CARE

Government-controlled healthcare was passed in March 2010 in the United States. Hopefully it will be repealed, partly or wholly, before it goes into full gear in 2014. An examination of how socialized health care works in Sweden can be a good motivator for such efforts.

In many instances, government involvement in people's lives does more harm than good. It taxes away jobs and gives some people the illusion of getting out of a cash-strapped life by handing them entitlement checks. In reality, their cash shortage has not changed; they now depend in part on their neighbors for their extra margin, a dependency they did not have before the welfare state.

The same goes for socialized health care. Such a system does not provide more health care to more people; at best, it redistributes health care from some people to others. Government makes promises about access to health care, promises that people accept and adjust their lives to. When the government eventually discovers it does not have the cash necessary to fulfill its health-care obligations, it begins defaulting on its promises and subsequently changes the rules of the game so it can deny people the health care they were promised.

Denials of health care always hit those who are worst off in our society: low-income people who truly believed that the government was going to give them a break. And the poorer a society gets, the more people fall into that category. The more people who depend critically on the welfare state, the more people will fall victims to its dark side.

### In the government's good hands

The 1975 film, "Monty Python and the Holy Grail", features a scene where two men walk through a plague-ridden medieval village. One pulls a wagon full of bodies and the other rings a bell and bawls: "Bring out your dead!"

They do not need corpse collectors in Sweden, at least not yet. But with the current death toll at the nation's hospitals they are not far off. Every year 3,000 Swedes die as a direct result of health care rationing and budget cuts in the country's single-payer system.[32] Adjusted for population, this death toll is at least 43 percent higher than in the American health care system.[33] The Swedish health care system is suffering under systemic rationing. Therefore, it is fair to conclude that should America adopt the Swedish health care system, the death toll would go up accordingly. This would result in the death of 274 Americans every day, or 100,000 patients each year – an increase, as mentioned, by 43 percent.

That is a horrible number in itself. But at least as horrible are the circumstances and causes of these deaths.

Such was the case of Mirabell, a happy little 18-month-old girl. She lived with her older sister and parents in Stockholm, Sweden's capital, which boasts a metropolitan-area population of 2 million. Both Mirabell's parents are non-doctor medical professionals.

In December 2008, Mirabell developed a fever that would not go away.[34] Her parents quickly realized that this was something out of the ordinary, prompting them to seek help at the Astrid Lindgren Children's Hospital (a part of the bigger, government-owned multi-hospital Karolinska conglomerate). When they got there, Mirabell had a fever of 105.8F. A doctor diagnosed her with pneumonia. After

X-rays, Mirabell was admitted and put on intravenous fluids and antibiotics.

This should have been the end of the story. There should have been no further complications. And even if there were, Mirabell's life should never have been in any danger. Unfortunately, this all happened within Sweden's socialized health care system.

On her first day as an in-patient, Mirabel's condition worsened. A "quick CRP" test was performed and she received morphine to quell the pain.

On the second day, a doctor concerned that Mirabell is pale orders a blood test to find out if she has anything more than a regular infection. No one arrives to take the blood sample, and, as a result, Mirabell's parents witness the deterioration of their daughter's condition. After a long search to find someone from the medical staff, the father finally locates a nurse, who, to his amazement, shows no interest in answering any questions. More likely, she stonewalls him because she has absolutely no time to set aside for him and his daughter.

Toward the end of day two Mirabell stopped passing urine, began vomiting blood and experienced breathing difficulties. A physician is summoned, but no further action is taken.

Yes. That is correct. Despite the absolutely desperate condition of this little 18-month old toddler, not one member of the medical staff – doctor, nurse or nurse assistant – does anything to help her.

This is unconscionable and, to many Americans, an entirely unbelievable scene. It must be an isolated, absurd exception from an otherwise well-working health care system, right?

Not so. First of all, as mentioned more than 3,000 Swedes die every year for lack of proper treatment within the government's tax-funded health care monopoly. The government has no choice but to underfund its hospitals because its welfare state puts such an enormous tax burden on the shoulders of Sweden's taxpayers. As a result, healthcare and nearly everything else in the economy basically grinds to a halt.[35]

High taxes result in smaller tax revenues.[36] Smaller tax revenues normally motivate politicians to raise taxes, but when your taxes are already highest in the world you understandably balk at trying to raise them again. The other option is to cut spending, but since they are ideologically married to maintaining a big government, such cuts will not end government spending programs. Instead, the guarantees ensured by these programs will slowly erode until they are entirely devoid of their original intent and content. And the high taxes will remain.

The government-run health care system is a case in point. Here, the erosion of the content means getting by with fewer medical staff and a smaller budget. To make matters worse, the budget cuts are not isolated to a year here, a year there. Instead, they become as perpetual as the high taxes and the government monopoly.

With each fiscal year, the government cuts away more and more resources from its hospitals. It assigns more and more patients under the supervision of ever thinner ranks of medical professionals. Those who are not laid off experience more and more stress. Their ability to care for their patients weakens with every staff cut. At some point medical professionals are forced to make a personal choice: do they quit before they get emotionally numb and stop caring about their patients, or do they stay put and do as best they can?

If, as in Sweden, the enormous taxes have basically destroyed economic opportunities throughout the economy, the choice is simple: be happy you have a job. So in order to survive a regular work day the medical staff simply ignore the screaming needs they cannot do anything about. As a result, a little girl of 18 months vomits blood without getting any medical attention.

The day after Mirabell vomited blood, her father displayed the stained sheet to a physician who made a routine checkup visit. Desperately, the father asked: "Is this normal?"

Still no reaction. Only after Mirabell suffered a seizure and her heart stopped beating is something done. She is revived, but it is too late. Her inner organs shut down one by one, and she is pronounced dead three days later.

Mirabell's case is any parent's absolute nightmare, and using it to gain political points might be viewed as crass. However, when her death is the result of a deliberate political strategy; when politicians decide that they want to keep the government's health care monopoly at any cost; when they put their ideology above the health and lives of the people they govern, then a tragedy like Mirabell's death becomes political. It is turned into politics by those whose legislative decisions deprived her parents of the freedom and choice to find and provide the best care possible for their child.

The tragedy of socialized health care neither stopped nor started with Mirabell. She was just one of thousands of patients whose lives ended prematurely that year. And right there, right at the moment when the ideological preferences of a nation's politicians cause another death of a patient in their monopolized health care system, the dark side of the welfare state casts its grim shadow over each and every citizen.

Many will still not believe that Mirabell's death was part of a pattern. They will prefer to believe that it was an entirely isolated tragedy. Numbers are abstract and do not come to life unless coupled with the faces of those who tally up to that number.

Therefore, it is instructive to go through some randomly selected cases of people who have died in Sweden's health care system. Their deaths illustrate the price that people pay for rationing, budget cuts, staff shortage and overall organizational stress in a government-run, tax-paid health care system.

> March 2007. A 75-year-old woman in the town of Sunne sought medical help for serious stomach pain.[37] She was constipated and vomited. At the only doctor's clinic in town, run by the government, she was prescribed laxatives. But the problem did not go away. She could hardly eat or drink and gradually got worse. When she came back to the health

clinic she was prescribed more laxatives. By early June she had barely been able to eat for three months. Her daughter drove her to the nearest emergency room, some 45 minutes away. Despite desperate pleas, the elderly woman was denied admission and told she only had a simple stomach bug. A doctor, who had no time to examine her, told her to eat bananas for dietary balance. A few days later, during a visit in a nearby city, she fell so ill she was rushed to the hospital by ambulance. She was finally diagnosed with the cancer she had been suffering from all along. It was too late though: she died a few days later.

Fall 2007. A woman with blood in her urine sought medical help.[38] One doctor assumed she has eaten red beets; another scheduled her for uterine prolapse surgery. During the surgery it's discovered thatt the woman does not suffer from uterine prolapse, but instead is afflicted with bladder cancer. Due to excessive waiting lists for surgery, it takes a full year before she is referred to surgery. However, as a result of the wait, the cancer has metastasized. Due to high staff turnover, the hospital cannot put together a consistent treatment plan. The woman dies 64 years old.

July 2008. In Gothenburg, Sweden's second largest city and home to more than half-a-million people, a woman was rushed to the hospital with an acute form of ileus (an intestinal obstruction).[39] The ER where she arrived was part of one of Sweden's largest, best-equipped research hospitals, Sahlgrenska, affiliated with the medical school of the University of Gothenburg. But after years of budget cuts the hospital, one of three in a city of 500,000 people, had only two operating rooms. Two elective surgeries were under way and the hospital lacked excess capacity. It took seven hours before her surgery could begin. By that time her condition had worsened beyond the point where her life could be saved.

<u>March 2009</u>. Lucas, four-years-old, also in Gothenburg, suffers from stomach problems.[40] He is initially diagnosed with constipation, despite his mother saying her son was not constipated. She persuaded doctors to further examine Lucas, and X-rays were taken. Doctors still could not explain Lucas's pains. They repeat X-rays on four different occasions but never order CAT scans, as those are considered too expensive. The doctors never had time to search for an explanation to Lucas's gradually worsening condition. Thanks only to his mother's desperate persistence a 3.5 inch tumor was finally discovered in her son's abdominal area. By the time treatment started, however, it was too late. Lucas died in his mother's arms, six months after she first sought help for him.

<u>May 2009</u>. A three-year-old boy in Stockholm was very sick to the stomach.[41] He had severe pains, vomiting, shortness of breath and lips turning blue. His mother followed a procedure that parents are commonly told to do in Sweden, namely to use the government's TeleMedicine service before actually going to the hospital. She described her son's condition to the nurse on the line, but was told her son had a normal stomach bug. The nurse advised the woman not to seek medical care for her son. Due to the serious rationing problems in Sweden's government-run health care system, employees at the Swedish also government-run TeleMedicine service get bonuses when they discourage callers from seeking medical help.[42] When the mother finally decided to go to the hospital with her son, it was too

late. He suffered from a severe form of bowel obstruction that had shut down the functioning of a large part of his intestines. He died.

December 2009. Micaela, a nine-year-old girl, came down with what seemed to be a toothache.[43] Her cheek and part of her chin had swollen up from the infection. Micaela's mother takes her straight to the ER in Norrkoping, a city of 120,000. Once there, though, they found that no one had time to examine her. The ER was not particularly busy that night – no major medical emergencies had happened, no major natural disasters, fires, airplane crashes or even major car accidents coincided with Micaela and her mother visiting the ER. The staff was simply stretched thin by regular demand for their services. Instead of a doctor, a nurse came out, looked at Micaela and suggested she and her mother visit a dentist instead. The dentist they saw the next day immediately sent Micaela to the ER at the university hospital in the nearby city of Linkoping where she underwent surgery for A-strep bacterial infection. To curtail the infection she needed to be put in a pressurized chamber; the closest hospital with such a facility was a two-hour ambulance ride away. By the time Micaela arrived there, the infection had conquered her body and she passed away.

January 2010. Marie, a 57-year-old woman with swine flu, contracted pneumonia, prompting hospitalization in Ornskoldsvik, a city of 50,000 in northern Sweden.[44] She was admitted to the intensive care unit, where an oxygen mask was applied. Marie's daughter explained to the medical staff that her mother possessed a phobic reaction to oxygen masks and required special attention. The staff had no one to spare for the extra attention and left Marie unattended. The next morning, a staff member notices that Marie's EKG signal stopped and the alarm attached to the unit has gone off. The staff member turns off the alarm but has no time to check on her. Another 35 minutes go by before anyone has time to follow up on the EKG alarm. It turns out that Marie removed her mask and detached herself from the EKG reader. She suffocated to death from lack of oxygen.

February 2010. A man in his 50s, diagnosed with osteoarthritis, undergoes successful knee surgery at the hospital in the city of Varberg.[45] The unit where he is being cared for is filled to the brim with patients. The lack of beds at the unit is, again, not caused by any unusual peak in demand for health care, but is instead the result of many years of persistent budget cuts. So the man who has just had knee surgery is placed in a staff room. For obvious reasons it is not equipped with alarms or any remote observation devices, which means that the man is left unattended for two hours. When a nurse assistant checks in two hours later he is dead from a heart attack.

February 2010. A two-year-old boy has been ill for a few days with high fever.[46] His parents realize that something is not right, especially since, for the first time, their son does not respond to pain/fever killers. At 4 a.m. they drive to the ER in the town of Mora. The toddler has a blood clot in his eye and spots all over his body. Despite this and the fact that normal medicine does not bring his fever down, a doctor concludes that he has a "normal virus" and sends the family home. They are told they can always return if the boy's condition worsens. "It was such an indifference and I will never forget it," his mother comments, well aware that she can tell the difference between a normal infection and a serious abnormality in her child's health. Two hours after returning home the parents notice that their son has cramps and is shaking badly. They return to the ER by ambulance. This time the boy is sent on to a larger regional hospital an hour's drive away. His condition is so bad that he dies soon after arrival. Later, his death is determined to have been caused by a meningococcal infection, with symptoms consistent with those exhibited upon his first ER visit.

The January 2010 case of Marie in the city of Ornskoldsvik is particularly illustrative of how the socialized welfare state ends up killing people. There is a direct correlation between the politically motivated health care monopoly and the budgetary measures put in place to defend that monopoly at all costs. Those budgeting measures consist of merciless budget cuts ordered by the county council; in 2009 alone the Ornskoldsvik hospital laid off 21 percent of its staff.[47]

The budget cuts were not prompted by any disaster to the local economy such as a mass migration causing a sudden plunge in tax revenues. As a matter of fact, the city of Ornskoldsvik has more going for it economically than most rural Swedish cities. The city is home to a multi-national corporation, an expanding university campus and a successful premier-league hockey team. But the reason for the cutbacks is attributable entirely to welfare state budgetary principles: the taxes needed to pay for a big, inefficient government suppress the tax base for that same government, thereby forcing the government to make cuts in health care – regardless of how much healthcare people actually need.

In a government-run system, not all patients die, of course. Sometimes the rationing of healthcare "only" adds insult to their injuries. Such was the case with Yasmine, a nine-year-old girl in suburban Stockholm.[48] She slipped while climbing a tree, fell to the ground and broke her wrist. An initial examination at the hospital led a doctor to conclude that, due to the severity of the injury, Yasmine needed surgery.

However, the government-run Astrid Lindgren Children's Hospital had no orthopedic surgeons available. At 5 p.m. in the afternoon, Yasmine and her parents were sent home and asked to come back 8 a.m. the next morning. Yasmine was instructed not to eat anything after midnight.

Surgery scheduled, right? Not so. Upon arriving at the hospital at 8 a.m. the next day the family found a long line of people waiting. No explanation was offered.

Three hours went by. Six hours. Eight hours.

After nine hours of uninterrupted waiting – 24 hours after their first visit to the hospital's ER – Yasmine was so hungry and so overwhelmed with pain that her parents pleaded for a dose of morphine to help her cope. It was not until 10 p.m. that night, 29 hours after they sought help, that Yasmine could undergo surgery.

There were no extraordinary circumstances around this wait. With apologies to Pete Townshend, it's just another tricky day for Sweden's rationed health care system.

A visit to the ER is not the only way where one encounters government rationing. In fact, it happens everywhere in the Swedish healthcare system. Swedes are discouraged from using ERs through the institution of high co-pays and additional steps, including TeleMedicine (which, as mentioned, has detrimental consequences) or "recommended" visits to local community health clinic. These clinics are typically understaffed and overwhelmed, often requiring day-long waits to see a doctor. Some of these clinics experience such patient overload that security guards are needed to keep patients calm or close the doors when the waiting room is too crowded.[49]

Even when you get to see a community health clinic doctor there is absolutely no guarantee that the doctor will actually examine you or your sick child – despite the government's pledge that everyone possesses the right to all the health care they could ever need.

A mother of a one-year-old girl learned the above lesson firsthand.[50] Her little daughter...

was passive and had a fever, and had been coughing for several days until she vomited … . [At the clinic] the doctor listened to her breathe and sent her on to have her temperature checked but refused, despite repeated pleas from the mother, to take any kind of blood tests. Instead the doctor diagnosed the girl with a virus and sent the family home with the advice to give their daughter fluids.

That the doctor did not have time to even check the girl's temperature is very telling of how overloaded with patients he or she was.

The next day, the mother, barely able to contact her baby girl, rushed her to the ER. Finally, she was able to convince a doctor to take a C-reactive protein test. Based on the CRP test results, the doctor hospitalized the toddler, provided her with intravenous antibiotics and diagnosed her with serious pneumonia. According to the doctor, the girl had come under care "at the very last minute."

These stories out of Sweden's socialized health-care system somehow escape retelling in the American media. So-called scholars at our universities, whose job it is to be impartial observers of their field of expertise, typically slant their research and leave out inconvenient facts and conclusions. Leftist agenda-pushers with access to the public arena somehow think that if they can turn America into some sort of European welfare state, heralded by socialized health care, they themselves will not have to pay the price of starved health care. Somehow they seem to believe that they can also escape other costs of the welfare state, such as skyrocketing crime, unbearable taxes and a lack of opportunities for their children.

They are wrong, of course, especially when it comes to Sweden. The country has the least accessible health care in the industrialized world, with outrageous waiting lists. These waits are the result of the government's cost-cutting measures, which in turn are the result of the government's own health care monopoly.

How do politicians respond to this? Generally speaking politicians are extremely reluctant to give up any spending program or admit that any entitlements they have put in place do not work as intended. Socialized health care is no exception to this rule. When the Swedish parliament, the Riksdag, addressed the problem of perpetual budget cuts and steadily deteriorating service in the country's health care system they passed a law that grants every Swede a health-treatment guarantee: no one shall have to wait longer than three months for treatment.

So first the government socializes health care to give everyone the right to health care. Then, when the government fails to deliver health care as it promised to do, it passes a law that gives everyone the right to treatment within three months. "You have the right to health care" says the government, "and if we do not give you what you have the right to, then you *really* have the right to health care."

We have already seen numerous examples of how this "right" plays out in reality. Here is another one. Mr. Ake Jonsson, is a 60-year-old man who broke his ankle on Christmas Day.[51] He waited for three months for word about scheduling surgery without ever hearing back. While waiting longer than the law says he shall have to wait, for the treatment he has the right to (actually, *really* has the right to), Ake limps along with a foot that angles 35-40 degrees inward as a result of a bone fracture.

Another patient that who did not receive what the government promised her is Mrs. Ulla-Britt From, a resident of the rural city of Ostersund (a county seat with 54,000 residents).[52] She went to see her optician for eye problems. Because you need a referral to see medical specialists, such as eye doctors, the optician sent the referral to the eye clinic at the local hospital. (Opticians are private entrepreneurs in Sweden outside the socialized health insurance system. Therefore, it is easier to see an optician than any medical professional.)

Soon after the referral was sent in, Ulla-Britt received a letter stating that she would be seeing an eye doctor within three months.

She waited. And waited. And waited. The three months went by. She did not hear back from the eye clinic. Four months turned into five months with still no appointment with an eye doctor.

Due to the government monopoly on health care no one can open a health clinic without the consent of the government. If the government says that there is no need for another eye clinic in the city of Ostersund, then there will be no other eye clinic, regardless of how high demand is for it.

After six and a half months and not a single word from the government-run eye clinic – and more than twice the waiting time than the government's own law proscribes as the maximum – Ulla-Britt picked up the phone and called the clinic. No one answered. She tried for hours every day for *several days* to reach the clinic, but no one ever answered.

### *Health care rationing – coming to a neighborhood near you*

The healthcare bill that President Obama signed into law on March 23, 2010, gives every American a guarantee that they will get health care treatment within 90 days.[53]

That's great, isn't it?

Only problem is – America currently does not have a massive waiting list problem.[54] It's the patients in government-controlled health systems that cope with excessive waiting for treatment.[55] Waiting times in America are only a fraction of what they are in countries where the government regulates and pays for most or all health care.

America's higher per-capita health spending not only keeps waiting lists down but also results in much better access to state-of-the-art technology.[56] While America patients take for granted their access to health care – whether paid for in cash or through an insurance plan – people in countries with government-run health care can by no means expect to get even an MRI or CT scan in a timely fashion.

MRI machines and CT scanners actually make good examples of medical technology that raises the quality of health care. They are also relatively expensive pieces of equipment. Therefore, when a government-run health-care system starts controlling expenses such formidable resources fall under the budget axe. Government-run hospitals and clinics either do not buy them or, when needed, postpone replacement far beyond what is medically reasonable.

In Sweden this has had a somewhat odd consequence. In 2005 the county of West Gotaland, home to the city of Gothenburg, considered shortening its long waiting list for MRI scans by sending their patients to veterinary hospitals for MRIs.[57] These are entirely privately run and funded in Sweden, which means that they offer state-of-the-art technology with immediate access. No one wants to keep his race horse or his dog waiting.[58]

The county eventually canceled the plan. Their motive was not that they themselves should be able to do the job in their hospitals; instead, they were concerned that if something went wrong while the patients were at the private facility they would not be covered by the government's insurance plan. If they got a reaction, for example, to allergens in a facility frequented by fur-bearing animals, the government would have to put up with all the related treatment costs, which could become expensive.

As funny as this anecdote might seem, it reveals the absurd logic and grim face of resource starvation in a health care system that has been run by politicians and bureaucrats for a long time. And resource starvation under the guise of controlling costs is the stated goal behind the socialization of health care, including the U.S. health care initiative. Politicians do not put it in those terms – their politically correct speak is "cost control" – but whenever costs for health care are kept down by political decisions, the immediate result is resource starvation.

Most people who seriously study the role of government in health care acknowledge this. A good example is a 2008 editorial in the Investors Business Daily:

> If universal coverage can work anywhere, it should be Sweden.... Yet problems there have begun to undermine a health care system that dates back to the 1930s, when

Social Democrats began to assemble a welfare state. Waiting times for care, long a problem in Sweden and too often deadly wherever they're found, are now the longest on the Continent, says European think tank Health Consumer Powerhouse. While Sweden "excels at medical outcomes," the HCP says in its Euro-Canada Health Consumer Index 2008, it is "really bad (and worsening!) at accessibility and service." [59]

And even the outcomes part is a false impression. When health care is rationed, only the patients in the worst conditions can get through. If you only treat those who are in the most dire need of treatment for any given medical condition, then obviously the health care system is going to look very cost efficient. The more pronounced a health condition is, the more tangible the results will be of treating that condition. It will seem as though people get a lot of health care for very little money.

But it also means that people will have to wait in line for health care until they are in bad shape. The price for that is paid by every hip replacement patient who can barely walk or sleep due to pain while waiting for surgery; by patients with deteriorating vision who will have to go almost blind before they are allowed to get surgery.

As is rightly observed by the Investors Business Daily, the government's motives for running its health care system are vastly different from those that govern free-market health care – and, one might add, the motives that drive us as private citizens to demand, or not demand health care:

> In private care, patients self-regulate and put less stress on the system. Thanks to the profit motive, private health care providers have an incentive to cut waiting times, lest they lose customers to the competition. Government providers have no such motivation. They do have incentive, however, to ration care when demand gets too high and costs soar.

But to do so exposes "universal access" and "equal access" to be inaccurate descriptions. "Restricted access" would be more fitting. [60]

This restricted access also shows up in cancer treatment in Sweden. Recently, two cancer patients described their frustrating experiences in an op-ed in Aftonbladet, Sweden's largest newspaper, in which they detailed the tormenting experience of having to wait for treatment:

> We who have cancer are always waiting in line for something. We wait first for the test results, then for the treatment to start. Then we wait for more test results, x-rays [then] the results of the x-rays, and we wait for follow-ups to see if the treatment has worked.... [I]t is a tormenting experience to know that you have a growing tumor inside your body that is not being taken care of. What if it penetrates important tissue and metastasizes untreatably?[61]

They also express frustration over not being granted access to state-of-the-art treatment methods and drugs:

> Every cancer patient must also be able to trust that she is getting the best possible medicine. We who have cancer search for every hope, no matter how small it might be. We search for every piece of news and every chance to get well again. It is absolutely cynical and totally unacceptable to be told that there is a medicine out there that has been certified for the form of cancer you have but that you may not get access to it.[62]

Restricted access to medicine is almost a trademark of single-payer, government-run health care systems. A telling example of how this works in Sweden is the experience of Mr. Dejemyr, a 20-year-old who

...suffers from the deadly Hunter's Disease [Hunter syndrome, a rare metabolic disorder]. His only life saver is a new medical treatment, but it is too expensive, according to the Karolinska Hospital [in Stockholm] which refuses to pay for it. "We just do not have the resources to pay for it. We could hire a number of physicians or nurses [for what the drug costs] if we had the money, but we don't," says chief physician Stefan Engqvist.[63]

To add insult to injury, the Swedish socialist health care system does not even let patients pay for their own drugs. Its denial of treatment, including access to medical drugs, is fair and evenly distributed across the entire population. If the poor guy has to die because the government does not consider his life worth saving, then the rich guy should not think that he can cheat death by buying his own medicine. Nor can the rich guy buy the medicine for the poor guy. A multiple sclerosis-stricken patient in suburban Gothenburg knows what this feels like:

> For each year MS-stricken Mr. Bengt A. in Savedalen gets worse. His doctor believes a new medicine could make him better. But the health care administration in the City of Gothenburg says no. The medicine is too costly. ... The medicine I am getting today costs SEK 15,000 [$2,100] each month and the new one would cost SEK 20,000 [$2,800]. I have offered to pay the difference myself, but was denied by the health care administration [on the grounds that] you are not allowed to do that.[64]

The explanation from the health care bureaucrats is that it is simply unfair to let a patient with money pay for a medicine that another patient cannot afford. Additionally, an individual who can afford the drug is forbidden from purchasing it for someone who cannot afford it.

In the name of some abstract, artificial notion of fairness Bengt is not allowed to buy a medical drug that would improve his life. The same ridiculous principle ensures Mr. D. cannot get medicine for his Hunter's Disease. One can't help but comparing this situation with the removal of all the life boats from the Titanic because not enough are available for all the ship's passengers.

The Swedish government can restrict access to medicine on a massive level because it has a monopoly on importing and distributing medical drugs. A similar monopoly will be put in place here in the United States, once a public option under the 2010 health care bill wipes out private insurance. (Yes, the public option is still alive and kicking! It was only disguised in the bill HR 3590 that Congress passed in May 2010.[65]) Since this puts the supply of medical drugs under the same cost containment principles as the rest of medical care, the government decides to deny people certain medicines because its bureaucrats do not consider your chances of getting better to be worth the money.

Restricting access at hospitals is not enough in Sweden. The country also has a Telemedicine service, an institution that Americans will in all likelihood become painfully familiar with under the "public option". In Sweden, the Telemedicine service officially provides medical advice as an alternative to visiting the doctor. Unofficially, though, Telemedicine participates in restricting access to health care. It pays bonuses to employees who discourage callers from even going to see a doctor. Reports the *Aftonbladet* newspaper:

> Send fewer children to the ER. And make sure the ambulance does not go out on emergency calls. Then the county administration in [the county of] Uppsala will raise your pay. 'I see no problem with this' says Mrs. Monika Maki Karlstrand, CEO of the Telemedicine service. Aftonbladet has seen the guidelines for pay scales that the Telemedicine board of directors in Uppsala county presented earlier this year. In order to earn a maximum number of points and the highest possible pay it was required of the staff that they: did not recommend ambulance more than in one percent

of the calls; did not recommend a visit to the children's ER in more than four percent of the calls; did not recommend a visit to the [general] ER in more than five percent of the cases.[66]

It is cheaper for the government to pay a bonus to its Telemedicine staff for each occasion they prevent a visit to the ER than to have the patient go in and receive treatment.

## Health care rationing in America: an experiment

To learn more about what "restricted access" really would mean for America, let us turn to history. We will do a little experiment: suppose that the federal government took over the health care system in 1970. Suppose that they had instituted all the cost control measures that comes with Obamacare and that the private insurance market would have given way to a "public option" that became the only health insurer in the country.

This experiment will show that:

- Americans would have paid much higher taxes;
- It would have been a lot harder to see a physician, a nurse and any other health professional – you would have had to wait in long lines;
- There would have been a lot fewer hospitals;
- Medical equipment and instruments, as well as computer technology used in health care, would have been of far lower standard than it is today.

Cost containment is a key factor in the push for a government takeover of health care. Proponents of a government takeover typically point to the fact that health care and health insurance especially becomes more expensive every year. Health care costs rise faster than our incomes and only the government, they say, can keep those costs in check. If we socialize health care, the argument goes, the taxes that pay for health care will stay unchanged forever.

So let us take them up on that. Let us assume that in 1970 the federal government took over the American health care system, and that one of the explicit goals was to contain costs. Just as with the 2010 health care bill we assume that there is no specific new tax that will pay for the new government program, but that health care is paid for out of the government's general revenues. (The 1993 Clinton plan wanted to impose a 7.1 percent payroll tax to pay for its socialization of health care.) Growth in health care funding is locked to the growth in GDP.

In order to see what impact this cost containment would have had on American health care since 1970 we need to determine: a) how fast health care costs actually grew from 1970 to 2008 (the latest year with reliable data) and: b) how fast they could grow when health care spending is tied to GDP.

Obtaining the first number is not difficult. We need only look at health care spending as reported by the National Income and Product Accounts by the U.S. Commerce Department's Bureau of Economic Analysis.

The second number takes a little bit more reasoning to find. Provided that the government does not change its tax rates, its revenues rise and fall with our income and spending. Our income and spending, in turn, are represented by the statistical figure referred to as Gross Domestic Product. The GDP figure is the sum total of all activity in our economy, so it covers every conceivable source of government revenues. It also represents all our earnings in all their various forms.

If the government wants to take over our health care system and pay for it through general revenues, and if health care spending is not supposed to rise faster than we can pay for it, then logically the government will have to make sure that health care spending does not rise faster than GDP. In other words, we can use historical growth figures for GDP to simulate growth in health care costs from 1970 to 2008 under a government-run plan.

We divide health care spending into four categories:

- Health care facilities -- hospitals, specialty clinics and all other facilities dedicated to the practice of medicine;
- Health care staff -- surgeons, physicians, physician assistants, nurses and others whose profession it is to practice medicine;
- Medical equipment and instruments -- surgery tools, laboratory equipment, CT scans, MRI machines, etc;
- Computer technology -- hardware and software, dedicated to use in the practice of medicine.

When we replace the actual growth numbers for spending in these four categories with growth rates for GDP the difference is astounding, as displayed in Figure 1 below. Each of the four lines shows how each of the four categories of health spending would change, compared to today, under a government health care monopoly.

- The dashed line, representing health care facilities, shows that over time we would not have accumulated any significant or even notable shortage in hospital buildings or other structures dedicated to the practice of medicine.
- The dash-dotted line represents the percentage of decline in health care professionals within the U.S. health care system under simulated socialized, cost-contained health care. By 2008 there would have been 31 percent fewer medical professionals available in the United States.

**Figure 1**

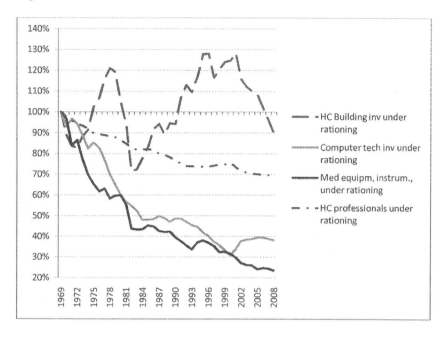

- The light-grey solid line, representing the difference in investments in computer technology, reveals that 62 percent of what was actually invested in 2008 would have been lost under socialized, cost-contained health care.
- The dark-grey solid line represents the difference in investments in medical equipment. At the end of the experiment, investments in medical equipment would have been 77 percent lower than what it actually was.

Two objections can be proposed against this analysis. First, a government agency running the entire health care system could make priorities between buildings, medical technology and staff. Thereby these numbers would, at least partly, be less dramatic.

In response to this objection, this chapter has presented plenty of evidence that in a government-run system such as the Swedish one, no areas of medicine, and no "inputs", are prioritized. Once cost containment is made a political goal, it supersedes all other goals within its jurisdiction. Once the government decides to contain costs in its health care system, that cost containment will become the guideline for practically every other decision made within the system.

Secondly, one could object that once the government is the only payer for health care it would be able to negotiate lower prices for medical instruments and equipment, and lower salaries for doctors and nurses. Thereby, one could argue, the losses depicted in Figure 1 would be much smaller.

One problem with this argument is that it also cuts the other way. If med-tech companies get less for their products they are less inclined to produce them and much less inclined to invest in product research and development. Private corporations are by far the largest investors in medical research[67] because they are naturally driven by their desire to make money on providing better products than anyone else. The government does not have such a motive and therefore has no inherent drive to excel at what it is doing. (Anyone who doubts the private sector's superiority in med-tech research and development should consider why the Soviet Union did not even come close to America in terms of state-of-the-art health care.)

With the private sector forced to sell to only one buyer at prices that far undercut market prices, there will be a shortage of research and development of new medical technology. The same goes for medical professionals. If the government runs the entire health care system and thereby can dictate salaries for health care professionals, the result will be fewer professionals and a problem with health treatment waiting lists that Americans typically are unfamiliar with today. Physicians in the United States are the best paid in the world[68] and consequently provide the best health care in the world. With cost containment methods in place under the 2010 health care bill, fewer students will seek careers in health care and fewer who already are will want to stay.

Proponents of a government takeover of health care, including President Obama, frequently deny that their reform results in any rationing of health care. Nor will it cause any waits for health care. These claims are, of course, bogus as we have already seen in the Swedish case. But the Swedes are not alone in having to wait for Doctor Godot. In 2009, Mark Pearson, Head of the Health Division at the OECD, succinctly summarized the waiting list problem:

> There are many good things to say about the quality of the US health system. It delivers care in a timely manner – waiting lists are unknown, unlike in many OECD countries.[69]

Another OECD report explains that while only one to five percent of all patients in the United States have to wait more than four months for elective surgery, up to 27 percent of Canadians have to wait longer than four months; in Australia 23 percent, New Zealand 26 percent and United Kingdom up to 38 percent.[70] For methodological reasons the report does not fully cover all OECD member countries, but those included all had wait list problems: Germany, Hungary, Italy, Netherlands, Norway, Portugal and Spain.

A third OECD report reviews waiting list studies from the 1990s and early 2000s.[71] The general message from this survey is, once again, that the United States never has and still today does not have a waiting list problem even remotely comparable to the problems in countries with government-run health care.

Even more damning for those who wish to let the government take over health care is what this third OECD study reports in terms of correlation between waiting list problem and the cost of health care: *countries without waiting lists spend 31-33 percent more money per capita on health care than do countries with waiting list problems.*

Interestingly, the countries with waiting list problems have different variations of a government-run health care system.

It does not get more obvious than that: when government runs the health care system, it prioritizes cost containment over patients' needs.

Against this background it is very disturbing that the "Obamacare" bill became law without even one of its proponents offering an explanation as to how the "reform" will keep waiting lists out of the American health care system.

The only way for the U.S. health care bill to avoid increasing waits is to keep the federal government from regulating the cost of health care. (This of course is antithetical to one of the key driving forces behind the reform.) But if the government took over the health care system without instituting cost containment efforts, it would be forced to raise taxes significantly. The dramatic inefficiencies that come with the government running anything will still be present. As a result, we the taxpayers will pay a lot more for something that we are already buying privately.

Regardless of the cost containment efforts, the taxes that would pay for an all-government health care system would be exorbitant. One way of showing how big this burden would be is to identify the share of a private employee's compensation that goes toward paying for government employees. Ultimately all taxes are paid for by private sector employees; when government employees pay income taxes they use previously paid taxes, namely the taxes that paid the salary of the government employee in the first place.

In Figure 2 the dark function shows the actual percentage of government employee compensation out of private employee compensation from 1969 to 2008. Over these 40 years the burden of government employee compensation has gone down marginally.

The gray function, on the other hand, represents government employee compensation as a percentage of private employee compensation if all health care professionals had been working in a government-run health care system.

**Figure 2**

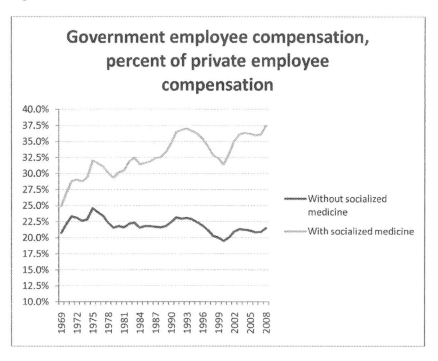

The difference is stark: already in 1970 government employees cost 4.8 percent more of private earnings. In plain English, this means a tax increase of almost 5 percent of your income – to pay for physicians and nurses alone. We have not even begun to add in the cost for health care facilities, medical instruments and pharmaceutical products. In 2008 the extra cost for health care professionals amounts to a whopping 16 percent of private earnings. That number is an average figure for all private employees.

Would you be willing to increase your income tax by 16 percentage points to pay for a totally socialized health care system that would not give you anything for which you do not already have access? It is important to note that if the government wants to *expand* health care coverage without causing any rationing, it would have to expand the number of health care professionals, increase the purchase of medical equipment and instruments and build more health care facilities. This would mean that the government cannot try to contain costs as promised.

On the contrary, health care costs would rise.

If all health care that is currently paid for through private health insurance is instead paid directly through taxes, the average taxpayer would have to dole out $6,600 per year in 2008 on top of his current taxes – or $13,200 for a family with two average incomes.[72] That is more than what the Kaiser Family Foundation reports as the average cost of a private family health insurance plan.[73]

Exorbitant tax increases like this would not come with compensation to employees. If employers see that their employees join or are forced into a public health insurance plan, they will automatically stop buying private insurance for them. But it is also unlikely that they will compensate their employees for any higher income taxes. Why should they?

The only part employers may return to their staffs is the part that is today technically considered to be an employee contribution. The aforementioned Kaiser study estimates that part to be approximately 27 percent, or less than $3,300 per year.

With the entire health care system in the government's hands, Joe Sixpack and his family, with two incomes, would lose a good $10,000 per year in net tax increases, *without getting so much as a dime's worth of extra health coverage for the money.*

Does this kind of tax increase seem entirely unrealistic? Politically, perhaps. American politicians tend to pay dearly for excessive tax hikes. But from a common-sense standpoint, as well as economically, the numbers are not unrealistic at all. In Sweden taxpayers shell out 12 to 14 percent of their income, depending on what city and county they live in, as a direct health care tax. And the health care system they get for the money is clearly substandard compare to the American system.

*Bare-bones health care*

Access to health care also depends on available beds. By international comparison, Sweden has few hospital beds per 1,000 residents[74] which results in patients being admitted to clinics that do not have the right medical specialty, simply because there are no other beds available.[75] Patients are also placed in non-treatment rooms, such as coffee break rooms or storage areas, which as we saw earlier can have fatal consequences.

Sweden also has the worst access to health care of any industrialized country, notably lagging behind even such a deplorably poor country as Albania.[76] Furthermore, Sweden is plagued by a lower survival rate in several forms of cancer than the United States, a fate Sweden shares with other nations with government-run health care.[77]

Perhaps the most damning piece of evidence that socialized medicine is not patient-friendly comes in the form of lethal injuries sustained by patients in care. As noted earlier, Sweden's health care system has 43 percent higher death rate than in the United States, adjusted for population.[78] Put bluntly: the United States stands to lose another 30,000 citizens every year if the government takes full control over the health care system.

Some of them may be lost from over-crowding of existing hospitals. When governments in charge of health care try to minimize costs they do everything they can to jam-pack all their health care facilities with as many patients as they possibly can. In the city of Malmo, Sweden's third largest, the university hospital is suffering from severe over-utilization.[79] Patients are located in hallways and offices. Even in dining halls are used, and even for patients with serious infectious diseases, including diarrhea and conditions that bring about serious vomiting.

A nurse describes the serious effects this has on medical safety and disease containment:

> The entire dining hall gets infected and it is not appropriate to serve food there ... Most of the time, though, there will only be a quick wiping-off of surfaces before the food or the next patient is brought in.[80]

Government efforts to keep Sweden's health care costs down manifests in many different ways. Emergency care is no exception. In Gothenburg the emergency medical services have stopped using so-called endotracheal tubes to secure airway openings for patients with heart failure. Instead they are using laryngeal masks.[81] The two devices have their distinct advantages, but the government-run ambulance service cannot afford to equip ambulances with both. Endotracheal tubes require staff training, something the government cannot afford. Laryngeal masks are also cheaper. The downside is that they are less safe in preventing a patient's gastrointestinal contents from reaching the lungs,[82] which has led to an increase in deaths among cardiac arrest patients in Gothenburg.

Cost containment even extends to x-rays:

> The five-year-old girl injured her leg in a bicycle accident. A twisted ankle, said the doctor. Ten days later it turned out the shin bone was severed.[83]

The mom of this little girl did not take her to the ER. In compliance with what the health care bureaucracy in Sweden wants people to do she went instead to the community health clinic. It was a doctor there who diagnosed her with a twisted ankle. No x-rays were taken to assure that nothing else was wrong with the leg.

> The five-year-old girl had gotten stuck with her foot in the wheel of her bike and the leg was severely swollen. Despite that the doctor concluded that it was just a twisted ankle and sent the girl home.[84]

When her leg did not get better, the mother brought her daughter back a couple of days later, with the same result: no x-rays, no further examination, and the same diagnosis: twisted ankle. It was not until 10 days after the first visit, when the girl was in so much pain she had to crawl in order to move around, that her mother finally was able to convince the health clinic staff to take x-rays. They revealed that the shin bone was severed, a simple fact that the physician at the community health clinic did not have time or resources to diagnose.

*Political smoke screens*

Laws against long waiting lists are useless in any health care system, especially one run by the government. Budget cuts at Sweden's government-run hospitals have now escalated to a point where they habitually violate the country's laws against excessive waiting times. The National Health Supervisory Board (*Socialstyrelsen*) has the national government's mandate to impose fines on hospitals that do not provide health care within the time frame stipulated by the law.

One hospital that has been fined this way is the Karolinska hospital in Stockholm. Serving the 1.7 million residents of the nation's capital, the Karolinska is actually a conglomerate of three hospitals with a total of 15,000 employees.[85] In 2009 the Karolinska cut away 900 employees due to budget shortfalls, on top of years of relentless budget and staff cuts.[86] As a result wait lists grew to a point where the National Health Supervisory Board imposed a 500,000 SEK fine ($70,000).[87] The hospital administration and the politicians who run the county of Stockholm decided that it was cheaper to pay the fine than to keep medical staff on payroll.

Yes, that's right! The county government in charge of health care preferred to pay a fine over having medical staff enough to cut its waiting lists. This is a case in point of what is wrong in the welfare state once it reaches the state of maturity where Sweden is today. Its taxes have suppressed economic activity to such a degree that tax revenues fall chronically short of what the health care system would need. Rather than acknowledging that the government cannot provide adequate health care, the politicians in charge perpetuate cost containment measures that eventually result in such absurd priorities as paying a fine for excessive waiting lists rather than cutting the waiting lists. Cost containment, not providing health care, becomes the prime directive of the health care bureaucracy.

This behavior obviously makes a mockery out of the wait-list law. It is nevertheless the grim reality in which Sweden's health care system operates – and it will eventually be the grim reality in which America's health care system will find itself, once government has taken over all of it.

As examples of how cost containment supersedes other goals in health care, let us take a look at two counties in Sweden. We start in Skane, the southernmost of Sweden's counties, with 1.2 million residents spread out over 4,200 square miles. Comparable in size to Connecticut, Skane has several cities, the largest being Malmo with a population of 270,000. Others are Helsingborg (128,000) and Lund (109,000) with the remaining 700,000 residents spread out over numerous cities and towns.

In an effort to contain the costs of health care, the county of Skane has reduced the number of emergency rooms in the county from eight to four.[88] Cities with as many as 38,000 residents no longer have a local ER. In some towns with 20,000 residents, ambulances have to drive up to 45 miles to the nearest ER.

A second example is Vasternorrland in northern Sweden, a county slightly larger than Vermont. There they have also closed ERs, which sometimes take on proportions so absurd, it is almost unbelievable. Suppose you closed the ER at the regional medical center in Rutland, Vt. Private citizens and ambulance crews would then have to drive 57 miles along the winding, mostly two-lane U.S. 4 highway to the ER in Glens Falls, N.Y. Suppose also that the speed limit never exceeded 55 mph and that snow removal services and road maintenance were at a fraction of what travelers using U.S. 4 enjoy.

This is almost exactly what people in Vasternorrland will be faced with in the near future. With 243,000 residents to care for, you would expect that the county council, with its monopoly on health care, would try its best to maintain medical services, especially ERs.

Not so. As a result of years of budget cuts, there remain only three emergency rooms in Vasternorrland, and that number could soon be cut to two. With 25,000 residents, the city of Harnosand lost its ER years ago. The county council recently released another dire economic forecast implying more budget cuts that verged on fiscal dismemberment of the health care system. And here is where the ambulance ride from Rutland, Vermont to Glens Falls, New York comes into play. In response to the new dire fiscal report from the county, three former hospital administrators seriously proposed that the county close one of the three remaining ERs.[89] This would force patients from the twin cities of Kramfors and Solleftea, with a combined population of 40,000, to go to the ER in the city of Ornskoldsvik – a 60-mile long drive that would make the ambulance trip from Rutland to Glens Falls seem like a joyride.

Given that the same county last year fired 21 percent of the medical staff at the hospital where the ambulances would be going,[90] one could almost ask if it would be worth the stressful ride.

Cost containment is so prevalent that even doctors and nurses are complaining, sometimes openly in the media. In many cities and counties, this is a violation of the conditions that employees are subject to under their employment contracts. Yet, a work environment where medical professionals are no longer able to provide adequate health care drives an increasing number of open complaints. One example is an orthopedic surgeon, Dr. Magnus Nordlund's op-ed in the newspaper Goteborgs-Posten in September 2009. He explains that the health care system...

> ...is increasingly dominated by authoritarian management with focus exclusively on the organization and the budget. [The management] is also characterized by a complete indifference toward the content of the care delivered, as well as toward the patients.... [The management] has also created a work environment where most staff members do not dare speak their mind: those who are audacious enough to sound the alarm about the deplorable conditions at the

hospitals are called 'concerned' and the management says they hope they will 'be more perseverant.'[91]

This is, of course, just another way of saying, "shut up and stop making trouble." Please note that this is the description of the government-run Swedish health care system as seen through the eyes of a senior physician at the orthopedic clinic at one of the most prestigious hospitals in Sweden.

Even the Swedish Medical Association has reacted. In the words of its politically moderated president, Dr. Eva Bagenhielm:

> At present the state of the health care system is strained, especially in primary care.... For many years the politicians have deliberately refrained from putting more resources into primary care. They have done so despite the fact that it is a cost efficient way to provide good health care. For this reason it has become increasingly difficult to recruit new, young physicians to clinics where their future colleagues are already staggering under their workload.[92]

The reason why primary care is not a prioritized area in Swedish health care is simple: There are no prioritized areas anywhere in the country's health system, whether it is primary care, oncology, obstetrics, cardiology, pediatrics or anything else. The only prioritized goal is cost containment, and the efforts to implement that goal reach across the board: no medical specialty is spared.

*How to handle costly senior citizens*

What kind of morality – what ideology – allows these political priorities to prevail? It has to be something deeper than just a destructive commitment to preserve the welfare state at all cost.

Before we get to that question, let me offer one more example of how desperately short on resources the government-provided health care system in Sweden actually is. In the Frolunda suburb of Sweden's second largest city, Gothenburg, elderly care is paid for and run by the government. The newspaper *Goteborgs-Posten* reports that the care facilities:

> …were so understaffed and so full of uneducated workers that the staff out of sheer desperation drugged the patients. Mrs. Christina Bohman's husband Leif was one of them.[93]

So here we have an elderly care facility, set up by the government, run by the government, financed by the government and regulated by the government; an operation that in every way, shape or form imaginable meets the left's criteria for perfect elderly care – and what happens? Forget care: the staff is so overwhelmed their only chance to keep up with the absolute minimum of their duties is to pacify the patients with drugs.

> Mr. Leif Bohman is basking in the sunshine at the Bjola elderly care home. Right behind him, also with a walking aide, his wife Christina is keeping a watchful eye on her spouse. 'He does not know where he is, but he is doing well now and then I am doing well, too' she says. Things were quite different in December [of 2008]. That was the first time when [Goteborgs-Posten] for the first time reported about then-77-year-old Christina Boman, who chose to bring her Alzheimer-stricken husband Leif, 82, home from the elderly care home Altplatsen in Frolunda, because she felt he was being badly mistreated.[94]

She reported her experiences to the National Health Supervisory Board (*Socialstyrelsen*) who actually investigated the case.

> 'I did of course hope they would investigate what was going on at Altplatsen. But I have to admit I was chocked to learn their conclusions' she says. Now the Socialstyrelsen has

published its report in which the frustrated staff tells the story about an unsustainable work environment.[95]

Mrs. Boman reacted in December 2008. This article was published in the Goteborgs-Posten in late August 2009. Over that period of time not one single politician voiced any concern whatsoever over what their government-run elderly care was doing to its patients. Not a single official admission of wrongdoing. The reason for this is not a particularly Swedish one, but rather something that is symptomatic for all liberal politicians: their ideology supersedes the results of its implementation. If they design policy based on their ideological preferences and that policy ends up causing a great deal of harm to people, then the liberal will rather defend his ideology than admit that his premises are wrong.

As yet another testimony to this ideology-over-reality preference, as of February 2010 the elderly care facility in this example had not been given more resources. It was still operating as if everything was working according to plans.

Because of budget cuts and endless cost containment efforts, Sweden's government-funded elderly care system can no longer afford health care to the elderly who simply need occasional assistance or supervision. Their resources and facilities, which were originally designed for light-help elderly people, are now swamped with older patients who require heavy assistance and lots of care throughout the day. Due to perpetual cost cutting, the government has replaced residents able to take care of most of their needs themselves with patients who require assistance for eating, hygiene and administration of medicines. Yet the staff is still organized around the light-care model simply because that is cheaper. Goteborgs-Posten again:

> Nurses and other medical staff did not have enough competence in caring for patients with dementia, despite the fact that more such patients have moved in to the facility.... The Socialstyrelsen writes in their report: 'The

nurses claimed that this had led to a situation where more narcotics-classed drugs off the approved list, as they do not have the skills and resources to do their job in any other way. This was not isolated to the Altplatsen facility as such, but applied generally to the Frolunda health district. In short: the staff was so short on hands and so poorly trained for the job that they pacified the patients with drugs.[96]

This elderly care system, paid for by taxpayers and overseen and run by politicians and tax-paid bureaucrats, was originally created with the best intentions in mind.

But why – *why* – does this happen to government-run health care?

# 3. FISCAL FASCISM: THE M.O. OF THE DARK SIDE

A friend of mine is a psychiatric nurse at a Swedish hospital. A while back I received the following email from him – just after the hospital management completed its accounting for the hospital finances:

> Yesterday we got a cake from the head of the clinic as an encouragement, and that's nice of course. But why did we get the cake? Had we provided more care to more patients and used more modern methods that had led to better treatment? Nope. We got the cake because the clinic had managed to reduce its share of the hospital's budget deficit more than expected. Recently the former chief operations officer at the clinic was fired for having systematically exceeded the budget. The fact that the number of patients seeking care here had increased dramatically was of course totally irrelevant.

Never during his many years as a psychiatric nurse has he been served cake by his employer for providing good care to many patients.

This little anecdote illustrates with cynical clarity what happens when the welfare state has reached the breaking-point where tax increases and as-usual growth in spending are no longer possible. It illustrates how politicians and bureaucrats permanently shift focus from the actual content of government spending into containing the cost of that content.

Once the welfare state reaches this point – and America is frighteningly close to it – the politicians who want to preserve it will never acknowledge that they have shifted priorities. They will passionately maintain that their main focus is on providing services and entitlements for people. But because it is no longer possible for them to raise taxes to pay for their spending, they will be forced by cold, hard economic realities into a choice between:

a)  acknowledging that the welfare state is unsustainable, or
b)  shifting priorities from providing services and entitlements to containing the costs of those services and entitlements.

It is almost a law of nature that once politicians have put a spending program in place, it never goes away. Therefore, the first choice – recognizing that the welfare state does not work and consequently do away with it – is out of the question for most of our elected officials. Rather than admitting that the welfare state has failed, our politicians pretend that it is still working well. They pretend that they will be able to deliver on all the promises the welfare state has made.

All they need to do is to make marginal adjustments in the budget. A little budget cut here, some reductions in spending there.

For friends of limited government this sounds good, like something that should be encouraged. The problem is that the adjustments – the nibbling away at the budgets for government-run hospitals, schools, income security systems, etc – are not motivated by any ambition to keep government limited. They are motivated by an ambition to preserve the very same spending programs that the government is making cuts in.

What is worse: the budget cuts that superficially look like an attempt to rein in government spending are not coupled with tax cuts.

This is the key indicator that our politicians are changing their priorities: from providing services and entitlements to containing the costs of those services and entitlements.

The combination of unchanged taxes and marginal cuts in government spending is not entirely new to America. However, so far our experience is that these occasional spending cuts are a rare exception to a trend of overall growing government spending. What will happen when the welfare state reaches the "Swedish" state is that politicians will make sustained, systematic efforts to cut government spending across the board, in budget after budget – and do it all without cutting taxes.

They will not do so out of political will. Instead, they will consider it a budgetary necessity. They will see their budget cuts as measures to preserve the government's spending programs and entitlements. Their reasoning will be something to the effect of: "If we slash away two or three percent of our health care spending this year, we will have a health care system that will fit within our tax revenues next year". But the reason why they do not have enough tax revenues for their spending is not primarily that they spend too much – it is that they have overburdened the economy with taxes. While spending is the reason for the taxes, the taxes have a direct, destructive effect on the economy. (Government spending also affects the economy negatively, but more indirectly than taxes.)

Since the politicians, in their effort to preserve the welfare state, do nothing to change government's destructive impact on the economy, the conditions that motivated their budget cuts remain. The cuts are therefore repeated the next year, and the next, and...

The Swedish welfare state has been subjected to systematic, across-the-board budget cuts for at least 20 years; recurring cuts in certain sectors began already in the early 1980s. This has led to the absurd situation where Swedes now pay the world's highest taxes but do not get anything more out of their welfare state than Americans do. A study by three economists at the European Central Bank shows that for every $100 that Swedish taxpayers pay in to their government, they get half as much back in the form of services and entitlements, compared to what an American taxpayer gets back on $100.[97]

This sounds absurd, does it not? Where does the money go?

I am the first to admit that the American government sector is not exactly a wonder of efficiency in itself. But because government is still relatively limited, it still makes relatively good use of the money we put in to it. The aforementioned study from the European Central Bank shows that government tends to become less efficient the bigger it grows. When government grows to a point where it can no longer pay for itself with tax increases, systematic budget cuts kick in.

These budget cuts reduce the quality and quantity of what the government gives back for every $100 of taxes. Since the price of the product – the tax – remains unchanged and the product is deteriorated by budget cuts, then obviously there is a corresponding drop in output efficiency.

Taxpayers get less and less bang for the buck.

## Fiscal fascism

When politicians do across-the-board spending cuts, repeated year after year, they do not have a malicious intent. Obviously, they think they are preserving the welfare state. What they do not realize is that they become trapped in their own vicious circle of never-ending budget cuts, never-cut taxes and an endless deprivation of resources in the government's monopolized sectors. Schools, poverty relief programs, income security programs, and under socialized health care all hospitals and clinics – the entire welfare state – are put on a reversed assembly line. Each year something is taken away from them: high schools lose specialty programs and extra resources for both bright and struggling kids; help to the poor comes with gradually higher eligibility requirements; income security programs replace less and less of your income; hospitals cut away helpers, administrative staff, nurse assistants, and slowly but relentlessly reduce the number of hospital beds.

Next year's budget will nibble away more. Schools make a habit of hiring unqualified teachers, whom they can pay less than qualified ones. Social workers demand more and more of the poor before they give them any help – they ask them to sell their car, all TVs except one, to cancel cable TV, to deplete every bank account, every retirement account they may have. Income security programs institute waiting times: you will no longer get your income security checks from day one, instead you will have to cover the first week or two yourself. Hospitals start closing entire clinics and patients have to make those long ambulance trips we discussed in chapter 2.

And the dismantling process goes on and on, but taxes do not come down.

But do politicians not see this? Are they not smart enough to realize that at this point the entire welfare state project has failed, is doomed and ought to be done away with completely?

There are two quick answers to these questions. First, as mentioned before, during the process when the welfare state is built politicians make a career out of liking the welfare state. Conservatives see it as a means to express their compassion; liberals see it as a means to redistribute income and wealth. And they both see the welfare state as a way to produce results, to show that they have "done something today". Some of them blatantly treat the welfare state as a machine for vote buying: you vote for me, I give you (other people's) money.

Secondly, once the welfare state passes the point where it is nice and benevolent, and it is put on that reversed assembly line, it will start fostering a different kind of bureaucrats. Once budget cuts become regular, cost containment has taken over as the prime directive of government operations. This is no longer a fun environment to work in for bureaucrats. Many of them will openly resist recurring cuts. To make sure the reduction in resources is actually implemented, government agencies will start recruiting a new kind of executives: those who are good at slashing budgets and keeping costs down.

As the government agencies are filled with managers and executives whose first and foremost goal is to shrink the agency's operations, they themselves perpetuate an atmosphere of cost crisis. After all, managing cost crises and tightening budgets is what they have made a career on.

The disturbing examples from Sweden's welfare state – both from its income security programs and its health care sector – are the result of this exact mechanism. Annual budget slashes are implemented by willing, career-oriented bosses in the government who learn, throughout their career, to have less compassion with the victims of their budget cuts than with their own careers.

As the reversed assembly line brings the welfare state farther and farther back into the realms of austerity and deprivation, the lack of compassion with those who have become dependent on the welfare state withers away. If people die in government-run hospitals, it is regrettable collateral damage in the process of executing the prime goal of the health care system: to contain costs.

This is the dark side of the welfare state at work. Its modus operandi is the combination of relentless budget cuts and destructively high taxes. Its morality is totally different than the morality of the benevolent side of the welfare state: people are no longer individuals, goals in themselves; they are irritating cost units.

Once our government starts treating us as cost units, fiscal fascism is here.

Unlike what is traditionally recognized as fascism, fiscal fascism does not have its own agitators. It is not an outspoken ideology. No one looks himself in the mirror and says "yeah, damn it, I'm gonna become a fiscal fascist."

Fiscal fascism is an unintentional yet inevitable – and *to some people* ultimately acceptable – way of running government. Fiscal fascism is used by politicians who possess perverted yet fundamentally benign intentions to save the welfare state. More than anything, fiscal fascism is the unintended consequence of concerted efforts by politicians to cure the illness that the welfare state has inflicted upon the economy.

For the reasons described above, once fiscal fascism and its detrimental consequences are facts, they become widely tolerated in political circles – even if there is not a single politician around whose intentions are malign. The vast majority of politicians will rally behind fiscal fascism because they have invested entire political careers in the welfare state.

## Under the guise of fiscal responsibility

Fiscal fascism's emergence and establishment as a leading policy principle was documented in the previous two chapters. Examples included the farm worker who was denied sick leave income replacement while struggling with leukemia; a woman grieving the loss of her son who was forced back to work the day after his death because the government declined to compensate her for lost wages; as well as every man, woman and child who died because they were denied treatment at a government-run hospital.

Sweden today is run entirely by the principles of fiscal fascism. It will become the rule of the game here in America as well, once the welfare state has grown to a certain critical mass. This is an almost mathematical truth.

Fiscal fascism is like an evil paradox built in to the socio-economic project of the welfare state. Once the taxes required to maintain a welfare state have been raised beyond a certain point, their weight on the economy cause two things to happen:

- The government starts experiencing chronic revenue shortfalls; as a result the government can no longer deliver on its promises to the public;

- Private sector activity slows down and more people than originally estimated become dependent on the government's entitlement programs, thereby driving up government spending.

When a nation comes to this point, its politicians are unwilling to admit they made a big mistake. Because so much of their political capital has been invested in defending the welfare state they seldom change their opinion – especially not publicly – just because they run into some funding problems. Instead, they dig in their heels and defend their failed policies.

One way that politicians can escape having to confront the evil nature of the dark side of the welfare state is to dress their never-ending cost containment efforts in more palatable terms. A favorite is "fiscal responsibility".

The technical reason why our politicians put the welfare state on a reversed assembly line is that of a government budget deficit. It is perfectly legitimate for politicians to try to close a budget gap – after all, we all know that it is a virtue to live within our means. Furthermore, with the recent rates of borrowing, the federal government is rapidly destroying its own ability to borrow money. Therefore, politicians who want to be fiscally responsible can make a good case for themselves.

The problem with fiscal responsibility as it is often perceived among politicians (and, likely, the general public) is that the term completely lacks ties to any meaningful political goal. A liberal can be as fiscally responsible as a conservative, or even a libertarian. They all want to balance the government's budget. But one wants to do it with uninhibited government spending, another wants to do it with moderately uninhibited government spending and a third wants to do it with practically no government spending.

Given how loose the term "fiscal responsibility" is, it can easily be used by those who are willing participants in running the dark side of the welfare state. When they executive destructive policies that kill people or leave them bruised and battered from entitlement systems and health care that was promised but not delivered, the willing participants among our politicians can justify their policies by saying that they are only trying to be fiscally responsible.

This is no fantasy scenario. This is how Sweden's political leadership has run the country for at least two decades now. Their version of "fiscal responsibility" is the "balanced budget". When I still lived in Sweden and was invited to lecture at the Riksdag (the parliament) among other places, I always made a point of asking politicians how they would handle a situation where they knew that their budget cuts – their efforts at balancing the government's budget – may cause severe harm to individual citizens. A common-sense answer to this challenge is of course to draw a line and say "no, I would never jeopardize the lives of people". It was scary to see that at best one in ten elected officials, holding national or local offices, would unconditionally come down on the side of the individual citizens. The overwhelming majority would find a way to answer my question in such a way that they could justify their budget cuts even at the expense of inflicting harm and suffering on people.

It is not just politicians who contribute to the perpetuation of fiscal fascism. By the time the welfare state starts deteriorating and sliding into its dark side, so many voters will depend on government largesse to make ends meet every month that politicians will fear losing elections if they suggest doing away with the welfare state. The general perception among politicians in welfare states like Sweden is that voters will want reassurance that their entitlements are safe. Legislators will try to convince voters that the budget cuts they make are indeed a way to save the entitlements. So long as they are successful the regime of fiscal fascism will continue.

Swedish politicians have become experts at this game. For at least 20 years now they have convincingly told the Swedish people that when they close hospitals, deny income security claims, reduce the quality of education in the schools and make harsh cuts in poverty relief programs, they are really just acting to preserve the programs, to save them in tough times.

### The media play-along

Convincing the public can be a bit tough, of course, if you have the media examining your policies. Again, Sweden has set the example of how the government can turn the welfare state from bright to dark without facing much of a public outrage.

During the 1980s when the first signs of systematic budget cuts emerged in Sweden the political leadership did an extraordinary job in rallying support for their policies. They were able to drum up support for their policies from media. They also found academic economists who were willing to render scholarly credibility to their "budget balancing" efforts. They also made sure to repeat their views on nighttime television with the droning relentlessness of an irritating wasp.

Media in Sweden, as in the United States, are heavily slanted politically. In Sweden, however, there is no Fox News, no New York Post, Rush Limbaugh, Sean Hannity or Michael Savage. Given how successful the liberals were in U.S. elections in 2006 and 2008, it is easy to imagine what they would be able to accomplish in the absence of any conservative media.

Sweden's politicians have secured control over the media through something called "press support".[98] This is an annual grant that the government pays out to newspapers, which reduces the pressure on newspaper owners to make a profit every year. Papers that would otherwise succumb to market forces are able to stay in business thanks to the press support grants.

In return for the financial support the press obviously does not raise any overly critical questions that leading politicians would be uncomfortable answering. The majority of Swedish newspapers receive press support; only the largest and most profitable papers remain independent, yet still rely on the supports as a cushion when times get bad.

In addition to subsidizing newspapers the Swedish government controls TV stations in part by owning them, in part by providing broadcast licenses. The first alternative TV station, TV4, is broadcasting under a strictly defined broadcast license that allows the license provider – the government – to raise questions regarding the content of programs.[99] At the point of license renewal, which is every six years, the government can refuse renewal if they think that the private TV station has failed to "consider the special impact of television with regard to the form and content" of its programs. The government considered not renewing TV4's license after a dispute with its owners. While superficially claiming their concern was the expanded ownership of TV4 by a major media group, it was widely known that TV4 had been too critical toward the then-incumbent socialist prime minister and that the government wanted to flex its muscles.[100]

As yet another example of how government controls media in Sweden, the Left Party launched a campaign against Fox News and succeeded in having a government agency shut down Fox News in Sweden.[101] This despite the fact that Fox News is cable-based and therefore does not need a government-issued broadcast license. The Left Party, which was known as the Left Communist Party until the Soviet Union collapsed, is itself affiliated with several newspapers that receive considerable amounts of taxpayers' money in the form of press support.

The bottom line is that Sweden's government has a tight grip on media within its borders. The American federal government enjoys strong support from the press without having to bribe them with money - provided of course that the president is a Democrat. But even if the press were to veer off its supportive track it would be easy for the government to step in and strengthen its ties to the press with the same kind of support as is provided in Sweden. This is particularly likely now that the press in general is not making much money. Once press support is a reality, any newspaper that is not unabashedly favorable toward the government would quickly find itself in dire financial straits.

This type of control over the media is as effective as it would be if the government took disloyal editors-in-chief out back and shot them. Political control can be exercised efficiently through a newspaper's accounting office instead of the board room.

Once control of the press is in place, the political leadership has one less obstacle to overcome as it employs the grim, ugly methods of fiscal fascism in defense of its welfare state.

*Government bureaucracy – another culprit*

In addition to the destructive interaction between government-dependent voters and re-election hungry politicians, the government bureaucracy itself is a culprit in perpetuating fiscal fascism. But it also deserves to be pointed out that the same bureaucracy is just as big a player in building up to the point where fiscal fascism takes over.

Just like private employees, government bureaucrats are interested in keeping their jobs. However, unlike private employees their fate is not decided by a free, open market. Instead, bureaucrats secure their jobs through something called the budget appropriations process.

Every legislature, from your local town council to the U.S. Congress, goes through an annual process to determine its budget for the coming fiscal year. This process should, in theory, be completely "new" every year, which was the original concept of the government budgeting process. This is often referred to as zero-based budgeting. However, as government has grown bigger and its payrolls have swollen, the practice of zero-based budgeting has ended.

Today the appropriations process that determines the federal government's budget, or the budget of a state or even a city, is vastly different. The normal practice today is that the chief executive of the government – the mayor, the governor or the president – asks his or her agencies how much money they anticipate needing next year. The heads of the agencies in turn pass the question on down through the bureaucracy. The individual offices within the agencies then respond with their "estimates," which are then added together and become the agency's appropriations request. Then the budget chief puts all the requests together and hands over a budget to the chief executive. He or she, in turn, brings the budget to the legislature where city councilmen, state legislators or U.S. congressmen make changes as they see fit and pass the budget bill into law.

Government budgeting is an issue that makes nine out of 10 people yawn and start searching their iPhones for something more interesting with which to preoccupy themselves. But by leaving government budgeting to the real nerds (yours truly being one of them) the citizen taxpayer, practically hands over his or her checkbook to the government. More to the point: the personal finances of the nation's citizenry are handed to the bureaucrats that crowd our government offices in ever bigger numbers.

By not bothering to learn about government budgeting, taxpayers leave themselves and their money vulnerable to the self-serving interests of employees in government offices.

If government bureaucrats had to compete in an open market for their jobs – just like we who work in the private sector do – then there would not be a problem. But when government bureaucrats can practically guarantee their own jobs by telling their boss – the governor or president you elected – just how much more they require for their little office each year, then the taxpayer is practically guaranteed to give just a little more to the government every year.

Ultimately, bureaucrats are only co-conspirators. The main blame for an ever growing federal government falls on Congress and the president of the United States. So long as they allow all the bureaucracies of the federal government to practically set their own budgets year in and year out, then obviously they also have to take responsibility for the results.

Their responsibility becomes all the more serious when the growth of government reaches the breaking point between the bright side of the welfare state and its dark side. However, it is more than likely that they will never see this point coming. When the bureaucracy can guarantee its own perpetuation through the appropriations process, and when conservative and liberal legislators share the ambition to grow government (albeit for different ideological reasons) then we have a perfect storm of coinciding interests that will practically guarantee that we will end up on the dark side of the welfare state.

### Coming to a neighborhood near you

America is entering into the dangerous territory of fiscal fascism. Both the federal government and the states are experiencing significant revenue shortfalls,[102] and the response is invariably to default on promises made to its citizens.

The true nature of every entitlement program is no less than a promise to the citizens. The government sets up the program and raises a certain amount of taxes to pay for it. As economic times get tougher, legislators raise taxes to pay for the same promise or cut back on the entitlements without cutting taxes; or both. Each one of these measures is a breach of promise.

Suppose that in 2010 your state government promises you an amount [E] of a specific entitlement (health care, education, housing subsidies). It also sets aside an amount [T] of tax dollars to pay for [E]. In 2012, when the entitlement program has been up and running for a while, the economy goes into a recession. Tax revenues fall. The state government responds by raising your taxes, but you are still only getting the amount [E] of the entitlement paid for those taxes.

Compare this to a car loan. You go to your bank and qualify for a $20,000 loan. You happily pay your monthly principal and interest.

You have an interest fixed for all the four years you will be paying on the loan. Then one day, when you are halfway through your loan, the bank suddenly calls and tells you, "We are going to raise the amount you have to pay back to $22,000." You get angry, of course, and tell them to take a hike. Then you read your loan contract and see that there is no clause in it that allows the bank to do this to you.

You obviously call a lawyer, whereupon the bank wisely backs down. After all, a contract is a contract. But the government does not feel it is bound by any such contracts with us. It can do exactly what the bank just tried to do: it can increase its taxes without providing a dime's worth of extra services or entitlements for the money. Or it can choose to cut the services it provides without lowering the taxes. In the bank loan analogy this would be like the bank, after having issued you a $20,000 loan, only allowing you to spend $18,000 of it on a car – they will withhold the rest and you will still have to pay them back the full $20,000.

We cannot classify occasional instances of breaches of promise as fiscal fascism. It is reckless, irresponsible and arrogant politics, but it is not a systematic abuse of government power. When, on the other hand, the government turns these occasional examples into systematic policy, the breaches of promise have become a deliberate policy strategy. When the government starts systematically breaking its promises, knowingly leaving out other policy options, it has stepped over the line into fiscal fascism.

So far systematic breaches of promise are not the norm for either the federal government or state governments. On the contrary, at least the federal government is trying its best to grow far beyond its means (another form of fiscal recklessness). The reason for this is simple: our government sector is not at Scandinavian levels. But it soon will be if Congress follows through on its intent to expand government.

Signs are plentiful, though, that state governments have already reached a point where they may step over into the dark side of the welfare state – into a state of fiscal fascism where ideology and bureaucracy conspire to keep citizens dependent on an ever more stingy government.

In Illinois, for example, some harsh fiscal choices await:

> In order to crawl from beneath crushing debt and reach fiscal solvency, Illinois legislators must choose from a series of options that range from bad to worse, according to a prominent watchdog group. The Civic Federation wants to launch an intervention that includes significant budget cuts and the largest tax increase package in Illinois history, all in an effort to save the state from a $12.8 billion budget deficit. "Doomsday is here for the state of Illinois," said Laurence Msall, Civic Federation President, to the [Chicago] Sun-Times. The group says it would support a state income tax increase from 3 percent to 5 percent. It also recommends the state tax retirees' pension and Social Security checks be taxed for the first time at the same rate as workers' paychecks. They want another $1 increase on a pack of cigarettes and to eliminate $181 million in corporate tax breaks. [103]

If this plan is enacted, the state government will deliberately walk away from its promises to taxpayers. It would do so while actually disregarding the privatization alternative. The state could declare that it is no longer able to pay for all its programs, return the money to the taxpayers in the form of significant tax cuts and seek solutions in the private sector of the economy.

If the state instead chooses to cut spending and raise taxes it would teeter on the brink of fiscal fascism by virtue of three steps:

1.  The government knows that it cannot expand spending anymore, even though both its ideology and its bureaucracy call for precisely that.

2. Both ideological preferences and lobbying from within government bureaucracies will assure that, whatever policy measures are taken, they will preserve the government's agencies and bureaucracies. In other words: there will be no prioritization between spending programs, entitlements and agencies. The government considers them all equally important.

3. As spending cuts are forced upon the government bureaucracy, they are spread evenly with each agency being asked to cut the same percentage out of its operations.

If this becomes a standing practice for running the state government, and no tax cuts accompany the spending cuts, then it has undeniably entered the dark side of the welfare state.

Ohio is another example where proposed budget cuts target everything from prisons[104] to libraries.[105] New Jersey is wrestling with an $11 billion state budget deficit and the new Gov. Chris Christie is slashing state programs. In California, citizens actually get to experiment for themselves on how to close the budget gap: the Los Angeles Times provides a "do-it-yourself" deficit eliminator online.[106] Readers can experiment with various methods for budget cuts (and tax increases) and come up with their own package.

The vast majority of states have indeed slashed their budgets across the board as opposed to prioritizing essential government functions. Observes the Center for Budget and Policy Priorities, CBPP:

> The cuts enacted in at least 45 states plus the District of Columbia in 2008 and 2009 occurred in all major areas of state services, including health care (29 states), services to the elderly and disabled (24 states and the District of Columbia), K-12 education (29 states and the District of Columbia), higher education (39 states), and other areas. States made these cuts because revenues from income taxes, sales taxes, and other revenue sources used to pay for these

services declined due to the recession. At the same time, the need for these services did not decline and, in fact, rose as the number of families facing economic difficulties increased. [107]

CBPP makes an important point in that demand for government services has increased in the recession. This increased demand makes the government's strategy to cut services even uglier than it otherwise would be. Cuts in services are executed precisely when people rely on them the most. They have not planned for their own income security, believing that the government will always be there for them.

But the mere fact that the government has to make budget cuts is a sign that not all programs are essential government services. It shows that the government has stretched itself thin over too many areas, that it is trying to satisfy too many of our needs.

When government is at that point, politicians have to make a critical choice: turn around and focus on the essential functions of government – or subject the citizens to the dark side of the welfare state by means of fiscal fascism.

# 4.  A RACE INTO POVERTY

Yes, this can happen in America, too. There are some eerie parallels between Sweden and the United States that should concern even the most passionate liberals. What should be at the top of their list is the fact that they will ultimately be responsible for introducing fiscal fascism to the American people.

One of the first victims of growing government is economic freedom. Normally – without government trying to do absolutely everything – we get to keep our hard-earned money and spend it as we see fit. But when government comes barging in to our finances, with do-good offers such as socialized health care and taxes to pay for it, we no longer get to spend our money according to our preferences and choices. We are forced to accept whatever the government gives us back for whatever it chooses to it take from us.

It is a well established fact that government gets less done with our money than we do. Among the myriad of available research is the aforementioned paper by three economists at the European Central Bank.[108] A compelling conclusion from their research is that when government increases its share of the economy from the average American share to the Swedish share, output efficiency falls almost proportionately.

What does this mean in plain English? It means that when you give the government 55 cents of every dollar you make instead of

30 cents, *you do not get a penny's worth of extra services* back from the government. The bigger government grows, the more it wastes. And while the government is wasting your tax money, you get to spend less and less of your own hard-earned money.

Let us put these two factoids together: more and more of our money goes to pay taxes, for which we get nothing more back; and your private consumption goes down because of the ever higher taxes. This translates into a lower standard of living, something that the left often smirks at but has a real, very tangible meaning to middle class families. Private consumption is not just hi-fi systems, nice furniture, laptops and flat screen TVs. Private consumption is also health care, housing, buying an environmentally friendly car and energy-efficient appliances, shopping for clothes and groceries that are environmentally friendly and brought to market with respect to human rights.

The left often touts this higher-quality, morally better lifestyle as a way forward into the future. But as anyone knows who has tried to live the environmentally responsible life, it does not come cheap. There is a reason why prices at Whole Foods and Wal-Mart differ. The more the government taxes earnings, the slimmer our margins. As our margins wither away under the burden of big government, we resort to lower-quality living. Consumer spending – usually the largest share of GDP – is suppressed and with it our ability to live responsibly and with quality. In the end, our economy moves ahead more sluggishly, jobs are lost and opportunities destroyed.

Figure 3 illustrates how private consumption in Sweden has tumbled compared to private consumption in the United States. Together with Figure 4 (coming in just a moment) Figure 3 helps us pinpoint the breaking point where a welfare state turns its dark side on its citizens.

Sweden's welfare state began exacting a burdensome toll on the Swedish economy in the 1970s. That was when Swedes' private consumption growth began a long decline: since the early 1990s private consumption in Sweden has not even grown by one percent per year:

**Figure 3**

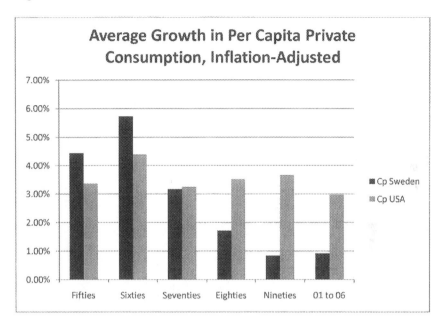

While Americans have enjoyed a reasonably good growth in their standard of living, Swedish families have practically not enjoyed any rise in theirs since the '80s.

The stagnation in standard of living reveals itself is many ways. One of them is the consumption of passenger vehicles. The median age of cars, light trucks and SUVs in Sweden is 50 percent higher than in the United States (and Swedish families typically own, at most, one vehicle while American families tend to have two).[109] Swedes actually have the oldest cars in Europe, with the exception of Albania.

It may seem superficial to point to the registration of new passenger vehicles as a sign of high standard of living. After all, liberals tend to tell us, there is more to life than money and what it can buy. But not only is that attitude the privilege of the independently wealthy; it is also an expression of ignorance regarding the consequences of having us all drive around in clunkers.

A slower turnover rate for passenger vehicles, results in longer waits for new, environmentally friendly technology to hit the streets. The same goes for buses used in mass transit. Sweden's comparatively large metropolitan transit bus fleet is a good example. New buses with energy efficient propulsion systems are more expensive than old buses with low-tech diesel engines. More expensive buses mean higher ticket fares, something people cannot afford if their private finances are squeezed too hard by taxes.

Car sales are obviously only one of many ways that a country exhibits its lower standard of living. Another is home ownership and construction of new homes. From 2002 to 2008, an average 24,000 new homes were built every year in Sweden, two thirds of which were single-family homes. During the same period the American housing market added 2 million new homes annually, with 85 percent being single-family homes.[110]

Swedes live in rental units to a greater extent than Americans do.[111] They also live in smaller homes,[112] have fewer children[113] and are less free.[114] All of this is directly or indirectly attributable to their excessive government.

America is on the same trajectory. We are about to permanently lower our standard of living without getting anything in return for the extra money we will be surrendering to the government.

Figure 4 shows how government outlays as share of GDP in Sweden grew during the critical period 1960 to 1980. The combination of government consumption and entitlement payments to households does not include corporate welfare and other transfers to non-household recipients. It concentrates entirely on spending programs such as health care, universal child care and tax dollars in our school system. This way, the trajectory in Figure 4 comes very close to the policies currently being unfolded here in America by the Obama administration.

It was in the period from 1960 to 1980 that Sweden was transformed from a predominantly free-market economy into a semi-socialist system with intrusive government and oppressive taxes.

**Figure 4**

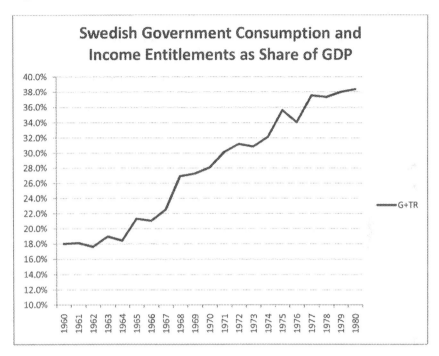

**Swedish Government Consumption and Income Entitlements as Share of GDP**

After 1980, when government consumption hit the 40-percent mark, the remaining free sector of the Swedish economy could no longer support the welfare state. One reason was that households now surrendered so much of their incomes to the government that private consumption suffered (as shown in Figure 3). With growth in the largest component of GDP slowing to a virtual standstill Sweden's private sector could no longer produce the tax base that politicians took for granted would always be there.

Instead of realizing their mistake, Swedish politicians desperately tried to defend their welfare state. By necessity they had to resort to the tactics of fiscal fascism. The welfare state stopped working for the people and slowly but relentlessly began working against them. It started punishing those dependent upon its benefits. Entitlements were cut, health services were cut, school children began experiencing budget cuts (when I was in high school we had "teacher-free classes" where we were supposed to teach ourselves) and law enforcement cuts resulted in a rise in crime.

Figure 4 is a harbinger for America. Figure 5 helps us pinpoint with good accuracy where we are today on the trajectory in Figure 4. Figure 5 shows total government spending in the United States, divided into two categories: government consumption and entitlement payments (remember – these are added together for Sweden in Figure 4).

America's government outlays rose to 30 percent of GDP during the Carter administration. It remained at that level through the Ronald Reagan and George H.W. Bush administrations and fell moderately as President Clinton and the Republican-led Congress reformed federal spending. Toward the end of the George W. Bush administration, government started spending more of our GDP. As indicated by the ends of the functions in Figure 5, we are now on a strong upbound path again.

The data displayed in Figure 5 is standard national accounts data from the Bureau of Economic Analysis.[115] It shows that in 2008 government consumption and government entitlement payments added up to 32.8 percent of GDP. This puts us perilously high on the trajectory in Figure 4 – the top, again, representing the breaking point where the welfare state turns from benevolent to its dark side and starts treating citizens as cost units instead of people in need of help.

**Figure 5**

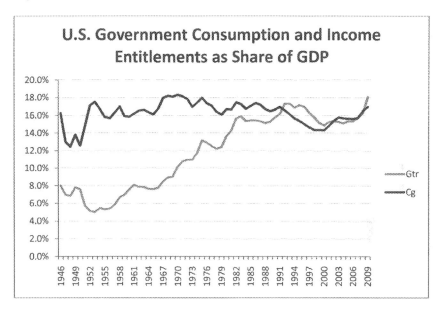

So what is the risk that America's government will grow past the breaking point?

One word: urgent. It is fair to expect that Obamacare eventually will socialize the American health care system. In order to measure the effect of that socialization on government spending we therefore add the health care currently paid for by private entities to government's share of GDP. Conservatively estimated, this increases the government's share of GDP by six percentage points. If Obamacare had been fully up and running in 2008, government spending would have been 38.8 percent of GDP instead of 32.8 percent.

A government takeover of health care is therefore practically all it takes to bring America to the breaking point. And we are already en route to that should all facets of Obamacare become enacted. But just to assure that we certainly will reach and pass the point where the welfare state turns dark, Congress could very well pass the FIRST Act or some similar act that creates a general income security program.

I find it hard to believe that any liberal (outside the most extreme circles who simply do not care what their huge government costs) has even attempted to estimate the cost of a general income security program in the United States. If they had they would turn away from it. The cost to taxpayers would have been $222 billion in 2008 alone.[116]

If we add together an income security program and socialized health care, the government's share of GDP rises to 42.9 percent, right where Sweden was in 1980. However, as Figure 6 shows, our government spending would have risen past 40 percent of GDP in 1990 had Obamacare and general income security been introduced in the 1980s.

**Figure 6**

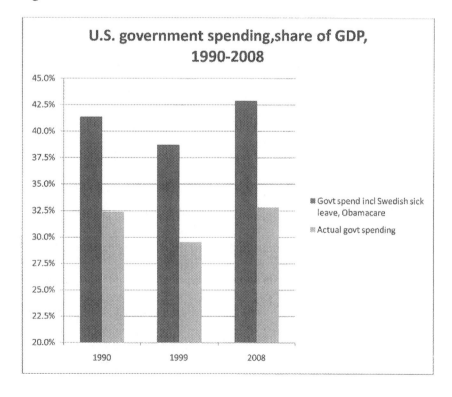

*The dark side – a real threat*

It would be a dangerous mistake to assume that the Obama administration is not going to pursue general income security programs. President Obama has vowed repeatedly to "fundamentally remake America"[117] and shows no sign of abandoning that commitment. There is no question that general income security is part of his "remaking" agenda. In fact, his economic adviser Larry Summers has made very clear that the Obama administration will make income security a "dominant priority" for the president's second year in office.[118]

Obama is under heavy pressure from such far left groups as the Income Security Institute[119] and the Center for American Progress, a well-established leftist think tank, to go in that direction. CAP's chief economist, Heather Boushey, takes every opportunity to speak in favor of the disastrous Swedish income security model.

Boushey's approach to income security is significant. Her prominent position at the Center for American Progress grants her direct access to the Obama administration. She also has a long background with other liberal outfits in Washington (such as the Economic Policy Institute), which provides her ample opportunity to testify before Congress and in other ways try to influence legislators.

It is important to understand how liberals argue in favor of a government takeover of our income security. To them, it does not matter that a government-run income security program has terrifying consequences; the examples presented in Chapter 1 of this book hold no interest for them, or else they would have discussed how to avoid similar results here in America should the same policies be enacted. Instead, they resort to primitive rhetoric that even tries to capitalize on the H1N1 virus scare to promote their ideology.

Let us listen to Boushey and her Center for American Progress colleague Ann O'Leary:

> Last spring, as schools closed across America to reduce
> the spread of H1N1, many parents had to choose between
> sending their child to a child care center, letting their child
> stay home alone, or even sending them to the mall and losing
> a day's pay--or potentially even their job--to stay home with
> their child. This is not a choice Americans should have to
> make.[120]

This is meant to be an argument in support of sick leave income security as proposed in the Healthy Families Act. (The FIRST Act is the most devastating, but far from the only income security bill circulating on Capitol Hill.) But first of all, the Swedish template that liberals point to as their model does not allow parents to stay home with their kids when their schools are closed. It is simply considered too frivolous of a benefit for inclusion in any bill drafted by Congress. And with a $222 billion price tag for an American program that just provides sick leave income security, it would be interesting to see where Boushey and O'Leary are going to find the money to pay parents when schools are closed.

Besides, if parents are going to be entitled to checks from taxpayers just because school is closed, then how many parents are going work during the summer months?

Furthermore, misty-eyed stories about an occasional hard choice for parents will not do American families any good. All of us who are parents know that it takes planning, networking and prudence with money to be a parent – but we also know that if we plan, network and are thrifty we can face unexpected situations without having to ask our neighbors (a.k.a. taxpayers) to chip in.

Parents know well that children above a certain age can manage a day at home alone. Children, for the most part, believe a day spent home from school is exciting because they can watch TV, raid the cookie jar and play computer games as much as they want, without their parents being able to say a word about it. Those parents who habitually send their kids to the mall when school is closed are likely to have a track record of bad parental choices. Their attitude toward their children and the responsibility of parenting will not change when taxpayers are forced to send them a check every day their kids are out of school.

None of this commonsense reasoning means much to advocates of tax-paid income security. Boushey once again leads the pack with a true-to-the-core socialist argument. Because some workers do not get as good employment benefits as others, she argues, government should take over and give everyone one-size-fits-all benefits.[121] The FIRST Act would do just that. In March 2009, Boushey testified before the U.S. House Committee on Education and Labor to suggest Congress pass the FIRST Act:

> If one was really interested in economic recovery, a policy that could get money to states while making long-term investments in working families would be the Family Income to Respond to Significant Transitions Act. I'm being sarcastic, of course. FIRST provides discretionary grants to states for the implementation of programs that provide partial or full-wage replacement for those taking leave for birth or adoption or for those who taking leave to care for themselves, their child(ren), spouse or parent with a serious health condition, as defined by the Family Medical Leave Act (FMLA). In helping to defray the costs of setting up these programs, the federal government can encourage states to support working families at a time when families especially need the benefit of paid, job-protected leave.[122]

One of the arts of being an adult is to balance income and cost of living so that one can build a buffer for occasions when one is home sick or providing care for family members with health problems. That is difficult to do when one is poor, but the FIRST Act is not for the poor. It is for everyone, including brain surgeons, lawyers and CEOs of big corporations.

These proposed entitlements would benefit every single U.S. citizen. In doing so, the FIRST Act violates the principles upon which the United States of America was founded: the powers of government were enumerated and specified in the Constitution to ensure that the government cannot assume unlimited powers. When the government creates an entitlement that covers everyone, it is unlimited by definition.

A general income security program would not be the first government reform to violate the limitations of government power in America. (Public education was the first.) But it would certainly be the largest this side of the socialization of health care. And its effects on the lives of Americans would be just as devastating as the same programs' impact on the people of Sweden.

*But wait: – there's more!*

As if socialized health care and general income security is not enough, another issue is lurking in the liberal shadows of Congress: a massive, government-run universal child care program. When Hillary Clinton was still a senator from New York running for president she supported the idea of government-run, universal child care.[123] As Nicole Gelinas explained in the New York Sun this idea has massive support from teachers' unions:

> And don't think that the teachers' unions want to stop at four-year-olds. In New York earlier this month, after heavy lobbying by the local United Federation of Teachers, Governor Spitzer signed an executive order that will allow 50,000 daycare workers who care for toddlers in their own homes to unionize and negotiate for higher pay and benefits.[124]

Even though former New York Governor Elliot Spitzer resigned his office, his plan to place government and teachers' unions in charge of caring for America's toddlers is alive and kicking. Boushey and the

Center for American Progress are fervent proponents of expanding government in general, and government-run child care in particular. She has been a leading advocate on this issue for a long time, making concerted efforts in 2003,[125] in 2004[126] and again in 2005.[127] Her work on socialized child care has been cited by the U.S. House Ways and Means Committee.[128]

The Center for American Progress is an important indicator of which way the Democrats are heading next. Therefore, their advocacy of general income security and universal, tax-paid child care should be taken seriously.

What should also be taken seriously is the literature that shows that government-run child care is, at best, a zero-sum game when it comes to child development. Notes a Danish study (emphasis added):

> Exploiting a rich panel data child survey merged with administrative records along with a pseudo-experiment generating variation in the take-up of pre-school across municipalities, we provide evidence of the effects on non-cognitive child outcomes of participating in large scale publicly provided universal pre-school programs and family day care vis-à-vis home care. We find that, **compared to home care, being enrolled in pre-school at age three does not lead to significant differences in child outcomes at age seven no matter the gender or mother's level of education.** Family day care, on the other hand, seems to significantly deteriorate outcomes for boys whose mothers have a lower level of education. Finally, increasing hours in family day care from 30-40 hours per week to 40-50 hours per week and hours in pre-school from 20-30 hours per week to 30-40 hours per week leads to significantly poorer child outcomes. [129]

Three Canadian researchers, who published their findings in the Journal of Political Economy (Vol. 116, Issue 4, pp. 709-740, 2008), evaluated the universal child-care program in Quebec. They found that having government involved in children's lives had very troubling effects:

> The study found substantial evidence linking the Québec Family Policy to negative outcomes for children and families. Parents reported a decline in outcomes for children on measures including those related to anxiety, illness, aggression, and motor skills. Parents self-reported a decline in health and their relationships with children and partners. Additionally, the study associated the Québec Family Policy with a significant increase in the use of child care services and participation of mothers in the labour force. [130]

Advocates of universal, government-run child care do not trust American parents. They neglect the fundamental fact that parents can make good educational and care choices for their children without the government's involvement. If a parent is informed (by, say, researchers at a think tank) that it is good for her kid to attend some kind of daycare, then she is free to make that choice herself.

# 5. THERE IS STILL TIME

Nowhere in the free world is the dark side of the welfare state more disturbingly displayed than in Sweden. Nowhere in the free world has fiscal fascism done more harm to people than in Sweden. It has dehumanized citizens, transformed them from individuals into items on a spread sheet; from independent citizens into cost units in a budget.

This dehumanization takes two outlets: high crime and industrial poverty.

*The seeds of dehumanization…*

Sweden has among the highest crime rates in the industrialized world.[131] That did not happen overnight. It takes time for a welfare state to deteriorate to the point where Sweden is today. Fiscal fascism is the slowly progressing venom that gradually works its way in to the very fabric of society. It leads to a systematic default on government promises. The result is on full display in Sweden, where escalating signs of social disintegration should come as no surprise.

When the first systemic budget cuts and defaults on promises came, people shrugged them off and dismissed them as a nuisance. Then things got worse. In the '90s the economy plunged into a sharp recession, brought about in good part by fiscal austerity. The very crisis it had caused led the government to accelerate its spending cuts. More and more money was taken out of circulation in the economy. The private sector suffered and the tax base was eroded.

Fiscal fascism went into higher gear, and the dehumanization of people accelerated. For every broken government promise more people were left short-changed and increasingly disillusioned and frustrated. Chapters 1 and 2 gave an account of people that have recently fallen victims to the dark side of the welfare state. They are not the result of some sudden change in government policy – they are today's examples of a trend that started more than two decades ago.

After the crisis in the early '90s, Sweden's government was left with a gaping budget deficit (does that sound familiar?). Its response, which should have been to dismantle the welfare state, was instead to take fiscal fascism to levels never seen before.

It is difficult to judge who in Sweden has suffered the most under the dark side of the welfare state, though obviously the poorer you are the smaller margins you have when the government starts defaulting on its promises to help you. Children of all backgrounds have also paid dearly for growing up under fiscal fascism. The quality of public education has plummeted. Schools hire unqualified teachers, cut support staff and demand that students buy more and more supplies themselves.

It is important to keep in mind that this is an ongoing process – not something that happens occasionally. On the dark side of the welfare state, government has put the welfare state on a reversed assembly line. As for schools, this means that budget cuts always are more important than spelling, arithmetic and history.

Perpetual budget cuts turn children into cost units. And they get the message. They build no loyalties to the society they are supposed to inherit.

*…and the harvest of social disintegration*

In the first chapter I gave an example of an arson attack on a school in Sweden. I pointed to the link between a destructive, malicious welfare state and the brutal expression of destructive desire among the young. That arson attack on the school in Rinkeby outside Stockholm is a drop in the bucket of ashes after hundreds of arson attacks on schools throughout Sweden the past few years. In 2006 alone, 505 public schools were burned to the ground or severely damaged by arson attacks. The year after, 439 schools were set on fire.[132] The trend has sustained since then.

This is what happens when children are denied the opportunity to build the ties of loyalty to their own society, their own future. When a society, represented by government agencies in virtually every part of your life, offers nothing but broken promises and treats its children as cost units, not humans, then that society deserves its burning schools and social disintegration.

Individuals who take to destructive social behavior are of course always individually responsible for their acts. But the government shares the guilt in some ways, as it deprives its young of opportunities in the name of the welfare state. It is the government that stifles economic freedom, that burdens the economy with enormous taxes and wastes totally unacceptable amounts of resources. So long as the government prefers fiscal fascism to economic freedom it is pointless to ask the children of the dark side to respect law and order.

The aforementioned 500 annual arson attacks on schools in Sweden serve as a grim reminder of what it means to disenfranchise, to alienate and dehumanize the growing generation.

In addition to burning down more than one school a day, Swedes also take the lead in disturbingly many crime categories.[133] Between 2007 and 2008 alone the murder rate rose by 49 percent, while other countries, including the United States, were trending downward. Adjusted for population, there are almost three times as many assaults and aggravated assaults in Sweden as in the United States.[134]

The parity is equally appalling for rape. While the official number for rapes per 100,000 residents is virtually the same in Sweden (30) as in the United States (32), American police can boast a 3.2 times higher rate of solved rape cases than their colleagues in Sweden.

In reality, the number of rapes per 100,000 residents is much higher in Sweden. The country has been singled out by the European Union as having by far the highest rate of sexual assault crimes in Europe.[135]

Emergency rooms in Sweden's two largest cities report admitting 600 percent more victims of violent crimes in 2009 than in 2002.[136] Armed robberies against convenience stores are also at epidemic levels. In Stockholm, e.g., some police districts report an 85 percent rise over the past couple of years.[137] Police districts in southern Sweden report an average increase of 106 percent in crimes against children (aged under 18) since 2005.[138]

Even the United Nations has noticed all is not what it seems to be in Sweden. The organization scolds the Swedish government for the fact that only three percent of all reported hate crimes lead to any kind of police investigation.[139]

Here is how the police in Gothenburg described a "regular" weekend in August 2009:

> Reports about shootings, cars on fire and gangs of unruly youth roaming around vandalizing [property]. The unrest in Hisingen continued during the evening and the night. "We have increased our resources and we have patrols out there" says police spokeswoman Pia Goksoyr. The police deployed extra units in Hisingen as a result of the attacks on police ... the previous Tuesday.[140]

Malmo, a 270,000 large city on the southern edge of Sweden, has been plagued by "French" riots for a longer time than French cities have. On a typical night during the summer of 2009, a dozen or more cars were set on fire around the city.

The following report is from Uppsala (160,000 residents) on the last weekend of August, 2009:

A police car on routine patrol was attacked with rocks and other objects. They called for back-up. When other units arrived the situation escalated. During the peak [of the riot] the police had ten units on the scene.[141]

When the clash with police was over and seven people had been apprehended and released, the police left the area. But the youth gang did not. Why should they? They had not really been reprimanded for their behavior. Later that night an RV caught fire in the area, as did two passenger cars. Cars are burnt on an almost a daily basis in Uppsala, according to police.

Let us go back to Gothenburg, Sweden's second-largest city:

The Friday night started out calmly in Gothenburg. Then came the incident reports from various parts of the city. Soon after 10PM two cars were on fire on Briljantgatan. Around midnight light rail trains [on line 7] were attacked with rocks. … On a train on line 1 two windows were smashed in the driver's compartment and one window in the passenger section. "We had to run for our lives to save the train and the passengers" comments Mikael Lagerqvist of the transit authority. The transit authority decided to cancel all service [in the area]. When police arrived at the scene of the attack they, too, were attacked.[142]

Attacks on mass transit buses and trains are disturbingly frequent in Sweden and often lead to disruptions of service, especially at night time.

Cars on fire, vandalism, arson attacks on garbage facilities, garages, schools… these rampantly anti-social activities have become so common in Sweden that the worst-hit areas are beginning to look like "a war zone" according to one resident of Gottsunda, Uppsala, a housing project that, for many years, has been plagued by nightly fires:

"It looks like a war zone. Our children should not have to see this when they arrive here at their kindergarten". Nick Leo, father of [a three-year-old boy], is upset. When children and parents came back to the Berwald kindergarten on Stenhammar Road in Gottsunda, Uppsala after the summer break two burned-out cars were the first thing they saw on the parking lot outside the kindergarten. "These cars have been here all summer. What is the city thinking when they let them remain here when the kids come back to their kindergarten?" asks Nick Leo. [143]

This image of two burned-out cars outside a kindergarten captures the transformation of a society on its way from a stable, norm-based life toward chaos, moral indifference and social disintegration. When I grew up in Sweden, seeing even one burned-out car in a housing project like Gottsunda would have been a sensation. Even one stone thrown at a police car would have made front-page news. Today, cars can burn every night in Uppsala, Stockholm, Sodertalje, Gothenburg, Malmo and other cities and the remains of those cars will not start to bother people until it is time to open the kindergarten after its summer break.

Not to mention the burning schools.

For the longest time nobody in Sweden talked about this collapse-in-progress. The primary reason is that many people associate the flashpoints of social disintegration with a high concentration of Muslim immigrants. Therefore, leading politicians fear that talking about the problem might create racism. This is changing, but too slowly to have any meaningful impact.

The political leadership is still inexcusably passive. Instead of assuming leadership and halting Sweden's slide into the dungeons of social collapse, the incumbent prime minister and his cabinet refuse to even acknowledge the situation. They remain passive, partly but not only out of political correctness; there is no doubt they are aware that any kind of concerted effort to bring the country back on stable, solid ground again would – yes – cost money. Rather than taking action by prioritizing law enforcement over entitlement programs, the government chooses inaction.

That this is a fatal choice for Sweden is painfully obvious. What is needed today in Sweden is not political correctness coupled with "fiscal responsibility"; what is needed is a government that is ready to lead the country out of its destructive spiral of fiscal fascism and the dehumanization of its citizens.

Especially the trend of accelerating dehumanization is a desperate problem. What better way to manifest one's loss of respect for human value, morality and empathy than to join those who actively try to hurt rescue workers during their attempts at saving life and property?

As a result of frequent assaults on rescue workers around Sweden they no longer go to certain areas of the big cities unless escorted by police. They know they might be attacked. A telling example comes from Uppsala, home to one of Europe's oldest and most prestigious universities:

> When the rescue service had put out a car fire in [the suburb of] Stenhagen late Monday night, a group of teenagers started throwing rocks at the fire engine so one of its windows broke.... The attack on the unit came when they were leaving the area; the rescue crew was not disrupted in their efforts to put out the fire. [144]

Attacks on rescue crews obviously open the door for serious tragedies. An apartment fire in the troubled suburb of Rinkeby outside Stockholm claimed the lives of several children. While the nearest rescue station is only a few minutes' drive from the address, the rescue crews had to stop on the way and await police escort. The reason is brutally simple: rescue workers are habitually attacked when operating in certain areas.

Not even sacred social institutions are spared. In Malmo a resting place for the dead has become the hunting ground for criminals:[145]

After a slew of robberies and threats the staff at the East Cemetery are forced to work in pairs – carrying personal alarms. "We recommend that no one come here alone on weekends" says the director of the cemetery, Malte Sahlgren. East Cemetery is situated on protected land, designed by the architect Sigurd Lewerentz. … [But] the peace and quiet that should characterize the location has recently been brutally disrupted. Youth gangs have turned the cemetery into a dangerous place for both the cemetery staff and the public. "I have worked in the cemetery administration since 1974 but never experienced anything like this. We just don't know what to do" says Malte Sahlgren. … "But I have lost count of how many reports we have filed with the police just over the past two weeks" says Anna Jeppsson, shift leader at the cemetery.

## *America on the brink*

The United States is perilously close to the breaking point where the welfare state will transform from bright to dark. The full implementation of Obama's health reform bill and the enactment of the FIRST Act are essentially all the ingredients needed. "Obamacare" and its public option – which is not dead, only dormant – will bring about a Swedish-style bare-bones health care system. The FIRST Act will take away people's ability and incentives to build their own financial security and socialize yet another dimension of people's lives.

Citizens will turn into wards of the state and be wide-open vulnerable to fiscal fascism.

That is not to say that we are anywhere close to where Sweden is today. The Swedish welfare state turned dark around 1980; it took a good ten years before its stinginess and its transformation of citizens into cost units and budget items began to seriously affect people's lives. It took another ten years before the signs of serious cracks in the social fabric began to show.

Theoretically, the United States has another 20 years to go before the destructive force of a crumbling welfare state sets in for real. In practice, though, it can go a lot faster. By international comparison our government spending is still growing fast. Minuscule complaints here and there typically are about a slowdown of spending. A good example is the reaction to Governor Christie's attempts at curbing tax hikes in New Jersey's cities and counties: loud complaints are being heard at the city level that they cannot frivolously raise taxes.[146] When property taxes have been rising at twice the inflation rate for a good decade, then a slowdown in tax hikes is perceived as a budget crisis.

Under the dark side of the welfare state, the best cities and counties can hope for is that the rate at which they dismantle services to citizens, year in and year out, might just slow down a little bit. The occasional cut in spending on libraries and the occasional delay of opening the public pool in a city in no way constitute the arrival of the dark side of the welfare state.

When the pool opens later each spring, and the library's budget is cut every year, then we are seeing the contours of the dark side. When school districts have to *actually reduce* their budgets by 2-3 percent every year; when Medicaid reimbursements to doctors go down every year; then fiscal fascism has just turned the corner and is heading for us full force. When the Social Security tax is rising as benefits are being cut on an annual basis; then we know we have crossed the line.

When the federal government fires bureaucrats instead of hiring new ones, but still raises taxes on you, then you know we are in trouble.

We do not know exactly when this point will come. What we do know is that we are heading for it, like a Titanic at full speed across the Atlantic. We know the iceberg is out there, waiting for us, and we know we are going to hit it – we just don't know exactly when. It could be four years ahead, but probably less. A joker in the game is the enormous federal fiscal deficit: it could force the government to go austere on all spending programs sooner than we expect. All this while trying to raise as many taxes as possible.

Once we do hit the turning point and our welfare state turns its dark side on us, we will rapidly experience the dehumanization that fiscal fascism brings upon us. And that will be a very ugly experience. What Sweden is going through right now gives us a hint of what will happen.

*What to do, where to go*

We are on the brink, but we do not have to choose the dark side of the welfare state. We can still put a foot down and turn around. Here is a to-do list that we can go through while there is still time.

1.  Turn "Obamacare" around. Our health care system suffers from an overdose of regulations, taxes on health premiums and compartmentalization of health insurance markets. By allowing people to shop for health insurance across state lines, by removing micro-managing regulations of how doctors actually treat us, and by preventing illegal aliens from getting unlimited access to our health care system we can bring costs down and significantly expand health insurance coverage.

2.  Return income security to the people. One of the most critical areas of our lives where a government takeover has very profound effects on our independence is financial security. The U.S. government already operates Social Security, the largest retirement system of its kind in the world. It is a system in trouble; thanks largely to 20 Social Security tax increases in 40 years the system has stayed alive for as long as it has. But the structural imbalance between tax revenues and entitlement payouts is slowly draining the system and will make it go bankrupt. The same will happen to other income security systems under the FIRST Act. A much better idea is to allow individuals to gradually be given

full control over their Social Security taxes. Each citizen is allowed to open a tax-free income security account: money paid in to it, equivalent to at least the Social Security tax our employer pays for us today, is not taxed, the balance is exempt from any wealth tax and interest on the balance is tax-free. Withdrawals on the other hand are taxed as income from work. A person who makes $36,000 per year would put in at least $5,400 annually. At a measly three percent interest the person would build a financial security worth more than $71,000 in ten years. This without investing any portion of it and, again, with an unfavorably low interest rate. Some smart financial planning and a good bank could bring that sum up to $100,000. Add salary advancements, career leaps and investment in retirement funds and even a low-income family can retire in full comfort without ever having to rely on the government.

3. <u>Put and end to Federal Aid to States</u>. The programs under this inconspicuous label represent the very core of welfare state spending in America. They range from WIC and TANF, which are genuine welfare programs, to No Child Left Behind and funds for boat safety education. Before the Obama administration temporarily but recklessly expanded federal funding for this cluster of spending programs with the $800 billion "Stimulus" bill, Federal Aid to States was sending almost $500 billion to the states each year. State legislators gladly accept these funds as "free money" that they pass on through entitlement programs, not realizing they are tying their hands when it comes to government spending. A dismantling of this entire federal welfare-spending conglomerate would allow states to take full control over their own spending. Thereby voters/taxpayers can come

much closer to the government that is taking away so much of their paychecks. They can more easily hold their elected officials accountable. Moreover, states have much tighter budget deficit restraints on them than the federal government and can therefore not frivolously expand government programs in tough times.

4. <u>A path to essential government</u>. Not everything the government does is part of its essential functions. On the contrary, very little of what the government does falls within its essential role in our society and our economy. In a genuinely free society government is confined to protecting life, liberty and property; to be the final arbiter of contracts and to provide national security. We have a long way to go before we get there, and chances are we never will. However, with this ideally free society in mind we can begin to rank government functions and programs based on how close to government's essential role they are. Once we do that, we know where to begin when we reform away government.

With these four points as our political cornerstones we can begin to turn around the growth of our government. We can begin to dismantle welfare-state spending programs that if left in place inevitably will bring about the dark side. But we must keep in mind that such an orderly retreat of government is only possible if we also cut taxes and give people back control over their own personal finances. Only then can they begin to appreciate private alternatives to government.

Throughout her history, America has overcome many challenges. The challenge of steering clear of the dark side of the welfare state is a lot bigger than most Americans realize, but it is definitely possible.

It is also necessary. In addition to Sweden countries like Greece, Italy, Spain and Portugal find themselves in dire fiscal straits. Their welfare states are less stingy than the Swedish one; they have in a sense faced the music earlier in their "career" of big government. But that only goes to show that the deterioration of the welfare state is hard to predict in terms of time.

The crisis of the European welfare state marks the beginning of the end of "democratic" socialism, radical liberalism and statism. It marks a historic turning point for collectivist ideologies. Most of all, it creates an unprecedented opportunity for governments on both sides of the Atlantic to end big government in an orderly fashion.

For America, it marks a historic opportunity to set ourselves on a course back to the principles the Founding Fathers laid out.

There is still time. Let's do it. And let us continue this conversation at larson4liberty.com.

# ENDNOTES

1. Aftonbladet, 2/9/2010: http://www.aftonbladet.se/nyheter/article6571965.ab.
2. The World Taxpayers Association reports: http://www.worldtaxpayers. org/stat_pressures.htm . Of recent, Denmark has marginally edged past Sweden, however this is primarily due to the introduction of new "employee tax deductions" in Sweden. These deductions do not reduce the formal tax burden but allow an employee to deduct a margin of the tax burden because he is employed. These deductions will partly be removed after the 2010 elections, should a coalition of leftist parties gain majority in the Swedish parliament.
3. The Australian company Rapid Intelligence produces a whole range of international comparative statistics: http://www.nationmaster.com/about_ us.php. A sample of what they report: per 1,000 residents Sweden has more than twice as many rapes as its Nordic neighbors; 1.5-2.5 times as high frequency of street robberies; 2-3 times as many assaults as other EU member states with the exception of Britain; and as much as six times higher violent crime rate than Switzerland.
4. For full text of the bill, please see: http://thomas.loc.gov/cgi-bin/query/ z?c111:H.R.2339.
5. Representatives (all Democrats): R E Andrews, T H Bishop, R L DeLauro, K Ellison, B Frank, A Grayson, R M Grijalva, P Hare, M D Hinchey, R Hinojosa, M K Hirono, R D Holt, M M Honda, C B Maloney, E Holmes Norton, J W Olver, D M Payne, C Pingree, S R Rothman, R C Scott, C Shea-Porter, F P Stark, P D Tonko, D E Watson.
6. Normally an unemployed person would be expected to get unemployment benefits, not sick leave income compensation. However, in Sweden one has to work at least six months full time to qualify for unemployment benefits,

whereas in the United States the right to benefits kicks in basically the moment a person is hired. Sofie was able to obtain sick leave compensation because she was caring for her gravely ill son.

7. Sick day leave

8. In the body of this text, "conservative" and "liberal" are used in the most common contemporary sense, and do not automatically refer to any particular political parties.

9. Klerman et al: *Welfare Reform in California: State and County Implementation of CalWORKS in the Second Year*; Appendix B: *Federal Welfare Funding after PRWORA*; RAND Corporation, Monograph MR-1177; 2001. Available at: http://www.rand.org/pubs/monograph_reports/MR1177/.

10. McCluskey, N: *Feds in the Classroom: How Big Government Corrupts, Cripples and Compromises American Education*; Cato Institute, Washington, DC 2007.

11. Available at: http://www.lawlib.state.ma.us/docs/DeluderSatan.pdf

12. Available at: http://www.lawlib.state.ma.us/docs/DeluderSatan.pdf

13. McCluskey 2007.

14. Day, John G: *Managed Care and the Medical Profession: Old Issues and Old Tensions*; 3 CONN. INS. L.J.1, 1996-97.

15. *Anchorage Daily News*, "Timeline: US health care legislation since 1798"; available at: http://www.adn.com/2010/03/23/1195673/timeline-us-health-care-legislation.html

16. Karl Marx's theory of the class society is the best known contribution. Its main point is that the capitalists unfairly short-change the proletariat for their work, thus implying that some, if not all, of capital income should be redistributed back to workers.

17. Tax Foundation: *Tax Facts and Figures – First Edition*; New York, NY 1941. Available at: http://taxfoundation.org/files/factsandfigures1941.pdf

18. Ebeling, R M: *Monetary Central Planning and the State, Part 13: FDR's New Deal*; The Future of Freedom Foundation 1998. Available at: http://www.fff.org/freedom/0198b.asp

19. *Social Security Act of 1965*; Available at: http://www.absoluteastronomy.com/topics/Social_Security_Act_of_1965

20. *The Kaiser Foundation*: "Medicaid: A Timeline of Key Developments." Available at: http://www.kff.org/medicaid/medicaid_timeline.cfm

21. U.S. Census Bureau: *Federal Aid to States 1998-2006*. Available at: http://www.census.gov/prod/www/abs/fas.html

22. Letter from Peter Orzag, Director of the Congressional Budget office, to Senator Kent Conrad, Chairman of the Senate Budget Committee, May

2007. Available at: http://www.cbo.gov/ftpdocs/81xx/doc8116/05-18-TaxRevenues.pdf

23. Please see: http://www.ntu.org/main/page.php?PageID=6. The National Taxpayers Union publishes annual data on how the federal income tax burden falls among income groups. Their most recent figures are from 2006, which happens to be the year with the highest concentration of federal income tax burden to the top ten percent income earners.

24. *TTELA*, 12/18/2009: http://ttela.se/start/trollhattan/1.678320

25. *TTELA*, 12/18/2009: http://ttela.se/start/trollhattan/1.678320-cancersjuk-kan-jobba

26. *TTELA*, 12/18/2009: http://ttela.se/start/trollhattan/1.678320-cancersjuk-kan-jobba

27. *Dagens Nyheter*, 12/2/2009: http://www.dn.se/debatt/svart-cancersjuka-kvinnor-tvingas-soka-heltidsarbete-1.1005929

28. *Svenska Dagbladet*, 1/13/2010: http://tinyurl.com/2cfqbek

29. *Svenska Dagbladet*, 1/13/2010: http://tinyurl.com/2cfqbek

30. *Svenska Dagbladet*, 1/13/2010: http://tinyurl.com/2cfqbek

31. Larson, S R: *The Swedish Tax System: Key Features and Lessons for Policy Makers*; Prosperitas, June 2006; Center for Freedom and Prosperity. Available at: http://www.freedomandprosperity.org/Papers/sweden/sweden.pdf

32. *Aftonbladet*, 2/9/2010: http://www.aftonbladet.se/nyheter/article6571965.ab

33. A study by the Institute of Medicine showed a death toll at American hospitals averaging 70,000 annually. The study is carefully examined in an article in the Journal of the American Medical Association, with criticism that the Institute of Medicine is in fact exaggerating the number of deaths: McDonald JC, Weiner M, Hui SL. *Death Due to Medical Errors Are Exaggerated in Institute of Medicine Report*. JAMA 2000;284:93-5.

34. *Svenska Dagbladet*, 1/21/2010: http://www.svd.se/nyheter/inrikes/foraldrars-oro-togs-inte-pa-allvar_4128019.svd

35. The only exceptions are major export-oriented corporations, but as is shown in Chapter X their relative success does not trickle down to the rest of the economy.

36. Laffer, A B: *The Laffer Curve: Past, Present and Future*; The Heritage Foundation, June 2004. Available at: http://www.heritage.org/Research/Reports/2004/06/The-Laffer-Curve-Past-Present-and-Future

37. *Aftonbladet*, 3/7/2008: http://www.aftonbladet.se/nyheter/article2002583.ab

38. *Hallands Nyheter*, 2/17/2009: http://hn.se/nyheter/varberg/1.389223-sjukhuset-kritiseras-efter-64-arings-dod

39. *Dagens Nyheter*, 3/13/2010: http://www.dn.se/nyheter/sverige/kvinna-dog-i-vantan-pa-akutoperation-1.1060591
40. *Aftonbladet*, 7/17/2009: http://www.aftonbladet.se/kropphalsa/article5524178.ab
41. *Aftonbladet*, 5/5/2009: http://www.aftonbladet.se/nyheter/article5075708.ab
42. *Aftonbladet*, 5/14/2009: http://www.aftonbladet.se/nyheter/article5142010.ab
43. *Expressen*, 12/15/2009: http://www.expressen.se/Nyheter/1.1814647/micaela-9-dog-efter-lakarslarv
44. *Aftonbladet*,3/11/2010: http://www.aftonbladet.se/nyheter/article6762922.ab
45. *Hallands Nyheter*,2/14/2010: http://hn.se/nyheter/varberg/1.733499-fick-vanta-pa-expeditionen-avled
46. *Aftonbladet*, 2/27/2010: http://www.aftonbladet.se/nyheter/article6690033.ab
47. *Aftonbladet*, 9/5/2009: http://www.aftonbladet.se/nyheter/article5744971.ab
48. *Aftonbladet*, 8/30/2008: http://www.aftonbladet.se/nyheter/article3210665.ab
49. Larson, S R: *Tales from the Health Care Crypt*; Journal of American Physicians and Surgeons, Vol. 13, No. 1. Available at: http://www.jpands.org/vol13no1/larson.pdf
50. *Skanska Dagbladet*, 3/24/2010: http://www.skanskan.se/article/20100324/MALMO/703249947/1057/*/svart-sjuk-ettaring-skickades-hem
51. *Aftonbladet*, 3/12/2010: http://www.aftonbladet.se/kropphalsa/article6763673.ab
52. *Ostersunds-Posten*, printed copy, September 24, 2008. Previously available at http://www.op.se/parser.php?level1=2&level2=6&id=954378; website only offers limited online archive.
53. Subpart C, Part I, Subsection 2708.
54. Available at: http://www.oecd.org/dataoecd/15/52/35028282.pdf
55. Please see: http://www.biomedcentral.com/1472-6963/9/1: "Waiting lists for elective surgery (WLES) are problematic for public healthcare systems, because patients often experience long waiting times with a negative impact on health and quality of life"
56. Available at: http://www.oecd.org/dataoecd/15/52/35028282.pdf
57. Vastnytt TV Station, 7/20/2005. Available at: http://tinyurl.com/269tadv
58. When I read this paragraph to my son he pointed out that the government in Sweden obviously should take over the veterinarian hospitals as well, and offer tax-paid insurance to all animals. After all, why should only humans have the privilege of rationed government-run health care? I replied that this might be an excellent issue for PETA and other animal activists to put

on their agenda, once Obamacare has done away with free-market, private health care in America.

59. Mitchell, D J: *Sweden's Creaky Government-Run Health-Care System*; Market Center Blog, Center for Freedom and Prosperity, February 2008. Available at: http://www.freedomandprosperity.org/blog/2008-02/2008-02.shtml#101 (original IBD link no longer works).

60. Mitchell, D J: *Sweden's Creaky Government-Run Health-Care System*; Market Center Blog, Center for Freedom and Prosperity, February 2008. Available at: http://www.freedomandprosperity.org/blog/2008-02/2008-02.shtml#101 (original IBD link no longer works).

61. *Aftonbladet*, 1/6/2010: http://www.aftonbladet.se/debatt/debattamnen/samhalle/article6382966.ab

62. *Aftonbladet*, 1/6/2010: http://www.aftonbladet.se/debatt/debattamnen/samhalle/article6382966.ab

63. *Aftonbladet*, 9/13/2007: http://www.aftonbladet.se/nyheter/article766763.ab

64. *Goteborgs-Posten*, 9/10/2007: http://www.gp.se/gp/jsp/Crosslink.jsp?d=113&a=368141.

65. In HR 3590, section 1334 does everything to introduce the public option except spell out "public option". Section 1331 says: "The Secretary shall establish a basic health program meeting the requirements of this section under which a State may enter into contracts to offer 1 or more standard health plans providing at least the essential health benefits described in section 1302(b) to eligible individuals in lieu of offering such individuals coverage through an Exchange." In other words: a public option. Furthermore, in section 2708 the new law prohibits "excessive waiting periods" for health care: "A group health plan and a health insurance issuer offering group or individual health insurance coverage shall not apply any waiting period (as defined in section 2704(b)(4)) that exceeds 90 days." Since America does not have an excessive wait list problem today, and since every country where the government runs health care has, the only rationale for this section is that the government knows what the consequences will be once the public option is reintroduced. The ban on "excessive waiting periods" was put in the bill originally because all countries with socialized health care have such laws (ineffective as they are). It remains in the bill to minimize the hurdles once the public option is officially on the agenda again.

66. *Aftonbladet*, 5/14/2009: http://www.aftonbladet.se/nyheter/article5142010.ab

67. Research America: *Rebuilding Our Economy: Investing in Research Critical to Our Nation's Health*; 2007 Investment in Health Research Report; 2008. Available at: http://www.researchamerica.org/uploads/healthdollar07.pdf

68. Please see: http://www.worldsalaries.org/generalphysician.shtml

69. Pearson, Mark: *Disparities in health expenditures across OECD countries*; Written Statement to the Senate Special Committee on Aging, September 30, 2009.

70. Hurst, J, and Siciliani, L: *Tackling Excessive Waiting Times for Elective Surgery*; OECD Health Working Paper #6; July 7, 2003.

71. Hurst, J and Siciliani, L: *Explaining Waiting-Time Variations for Elective Surgery Across OECD Countries*; OECD Economic Studies #38, 2004/1.

72. These figures are from the national health expenditure databases maintained by the Center for Medicare and Medicaid Services of the U.S. Department of Health and Human Services: http://cms.hhs.gov.

73. An annual survey of health plan costs by the Kaiser Family Foundation in 2007 found that the average health plan cost $12,106 per year, with the average cost increase at six percent per year: http://www.kff.org/insurance/ehbs091107nr.cfm.

74. *Goteborgs-Posten*; 10/5/2009: http://www.gp.se/nyheter/debatt/1.216713-nya-neddragningar-riskerar-varden-pa-su

75. *Svenska Dagbladet*;10/22/2009: http://www.svd.se/opinion/brannpunkt/slarvande-vardgivare-ska-botfallas_3687677.svd

76. Please see: http://healthpowerhouse.com/files/Sweden.pdf

77. Please see: http://www.ncpa.org/pub/ba596 and http://www.opinionjournal.com/la/?id=110009344

78. Please see: http://www.socialstyrelsen.se/patientsakerhet/vardskadematningar#

79. *Sveriges Radio Public Radio Station*; 6/15/2009: http://sverigesradio.se/cgi-bin/ekot/artikel.asp?artikel=2904127

80. *Sveriges Radio Public Radio Station*; 6/15/2009: http://sverigesradio.se/cgi-bin/ekot/artikel.asp?artikel=2904127

81. *Goteborgs-Posten*; 3/28/2010: http://www.gp.se/nyheter/goteborg/1.340238-ny-ambulansrutin-kan-vara-farlig-for-patienter

82. Please see: http://en.scientificcommons.org/55556793

83. *Lanstidningen*; 10/9/2009: http://lt.se/nyheter/1.591355-femaring-skickades-hem-med-brutet-ben

84. *Lanstidningen*; 10/9/2009: http://lt.se/nyheter/1.591355-femaring-skickades-hem-med-brutet-ben

85. Please see: http://www.karolinska.se/en/Karolinska-University-Hospital/

86. *Aftonbladet*;1/22/2009: http://www.aftonbladet.se/kropphalsa/article4236059.ab and http://www.aftonbladet.se/kropphalsa/article4237233.ab

87. *Dagens Nyheter*; 3/17/2010: http://www.dn.se/sthlm/stockholms-landsting-riskerar-boter-1.1062766

88. *Sydsvenska Dagbladet*; 3/10/2010: http://sydsvenskan.se/sverige/article636546/Sjukhus-maste-spara-halv-miljard.html

89. *Sundsvalls Tidning*;1/19/2010: http://st.nu/opinion/debatt/1.1731989-laggned-akutverksamheten-vid-solleftea-sjukhus

90. *Aftonbladet*; 9/5/2009: http://www.aftonbladet.se/nyheter/article5744971.ab

91. *Goteborgs-Posten*; 9/29/2009: http://www.gp.se/nyheter/debatt/1.213237-problemet-ar-en-likgiltig-ledning

92. *Dagens Nyheter*; 9/2/2009: http://www.dn.se/debatt/sverige-behover-akut-1-500-nya-allmanlakare-1.943175

93. *Goteborgs-Posten*; 8/27/2009: http://gp.se/gp/jsp/Crosslink.jsp?d=113&a=513602

94. *Goteborgs-Posten*; 8/27/2009: http://gp.se/gp/jsp/Crosslink.jsp?d=113&a=513602

95. *Goteborgs-Posten*; 8/27/2009: http://gp.se/gp/jsp/Crosslink.jsp?d=113&a=513602

96. *Goteborgs-Posten*; 8/27/2009: http://gp.se/gp/jsp/Crosslink.jsp?d=113&a=513602 and http://www.gp.se/nyheter/goteborg/1.13048-hennes-kamp-gav-resultat

97. Afonso, Schuknecht and Tanzi: *Public sector efficiency: an international comparison*, Research Report 2003:242, European Central Bank, July 2003. Available at: http://www.ecb.int/pub/pdf/scpwps/ecbwp242.pdf.

98. Please see: http://www.ts.se/Medierevision/Presstod.aspx

99. Please see: http://www.rtvv.se/_upload/tillstandsvillkor/TV4.pdf

100. *Sveriges Television Public Television*, 1/24/2005: http://tinyurl.com/y5rp7th

101. Please see: http://www.grn.se/grn/pages/CommissionPage   620.aspx?dnr=0723%2f2006

102. Associated Press; 2/23/2010: http://finance.yahoo.com/news/Report-States-tax-collections-apf-969834970.html?x=0&.v=2

103. *MSNBC News*, 2.25.2010: http://www.nbcchicago.com/news/local-beat/Doomsday-Taxes-State-of-Illinois-84947527.html#ixzz0l0mtrHVc

104. *The Columbus Dispatch*; 12/12/2008: http://tinyurl.com/69hm2n

105. WYSO Public Radio; 6/22/2009: http://tinyurl.com/lsu3jl

106. Please see: http://www.latimes.com/news/local/la-statebudget-fl,0,95571.htmlstory

107. Johnson, Oliff and Williams: *An Update on State Budget Cuts*; Center for Budget and Policy Priorities; 5/25/2010/ Available at: http://www.cbpp.org/cms/?fa=view&id=1214

108. Alfonso, Schuknecht and Tanzi: *Public sector efficiency: an international comparison* (Working Paper No. 242), European Central Bank. Available at: http://www.ecb.int/pub/pdf/scpwps/ecbwp242.pdf. Also published in *Public Choice* (2005), 123: 321-347.

109. Bureau of Transportation Statistics: National transportation statistics 2008, Table 1-25. Available at: http://www.bts.gov/publications/national_transportation_statistics/2008/html/table_01_25.html. See also: Statistics Sweden, Passenger vehicle statistics, available at: http://www.scb.se/Pages/ProductTables____10516.aspx

110. U.S. Census Bureau, residential construction data, available at: http://www.census.gov/const/www/newresconstindex.html and corresponding numbers from Statistics Sweden: http://www.scb.se/Pages/Product____5592.aspx.

111. Please see: http://www.nationmaster.com/graph/peo_hom_own-people-home-ownership

112. Please see: http://www.nationmaster.com/graph/peo_siz_of_hou-people-size-of-houses

113. Please see: http://www.nationmaster.com/graph/peo_bir_rat-people-birth-rate

114. The Heritage Foundation: 2010 Index of Economic Freedom; country ranking available at: http://www.heritage.org/index/Ranking.aspx

115. Bureau of Economic Analysis, National Accounts, Section 1; available at: http://bea.gov/national/nipaweb/SelectTable.asp?Selected=N#S1

116. The assumption behind this figure consists of three steps: a) the income security system replaces 100 percent of the wage earner's reported wage, as opposed to the 80 percent in the Swedish system; b) there are no "skip days" where the person on sick leave is denied coverage for the first, say, 2-3 days (the Swedish system has "skip days"); and c) Americans change their propensity to call in sick to mimic the propensity to call in sick in Sweden, and the federal government does not put any non-monetary restrictions in the way of this propensity shift.

117. Please see: www.**youtube.com**/watch?v=_cqN4NIEtOY

118. Steve Thomma and Margaret Talev: *It Isn't Going to be Easier for Obama in the Second Year*; January 15, 2010. Available at: http://www.mcclatchydc.com/227/story/82473.html

119. Steven Sharafman: "The dream, vision and promise of America includes income security for all"; *Open Letter to President Obama*; Income Security for All Campaign. Available at: http://www.incomesecurityforall.org/

120. Please see: http://www.americanprogress.org/pressroom/statements/2009/11/H1N1Leave.html

121. Please see: http://www.truthout.org/article/heather-boushey-no-benefit-jobs-leave-parents-struggling

122. Please see: http://www.americanprogressaction.org/issues/2009/03/boushey_workplace.html

123. Hillary Clinton: "Remarks in Miami on expanding Pre-K"; *The American Presidency Project*; May 21, 2007. Available at: http://www.presidency.ucsb.edu/ws/index.php?pid=77068

124. *New York Sun*, May 25, 2007: www.nysun.com/opinion/**clinton**s-**child-care**-flunks/55229/

125. Please see: http://www.cepr.net/documents/publications/child_care_2003.htm

126. Please see: http://www.cepr.net/documents/publications/child_care_2004.htm. Interestingly, Boshey notes that senator Olympia Snowe, RINO-ME, authored a proposal to add $6 billion in child care support to the welfare program TANF.

127. Please see: http://www.commondreams.org/news2005/0207-06.htm

128. U.S. House of Representatives, Committee on Ways and Means; available at: http://waysandmeans.house.gov/hearings.asp?formmode=view&id=2971

129. Please see: http://ftp.iza.org/dp3188.pdf

130. Miller, Gruber and Milligan: "Universal child care, maternal well-being and labor supply"; *Journal of Political Economy*, Volume 116, Issue 4, pp. 709-740. Available at: http://www.cecw-cepb.ca/publications/921

131. Please see http://www.nationmaster.com/about_us.php and Eurostat's crime database at http://epp.eurostat.ec.europa.eu/portal/page/portal/eurostat/home/

132. *Aftonbladet*, 1/29/2009: http://www.aftonbladet.se/nyheter/article4285361.ab

133. Please see http://www.nationmaster.com/about_us.php and Eurostat's crime database at http://epp.eurostat.ec.europa.eu/portal/page/portal/eurostat/home/

134. The Swedish National Bureau of Crime Prevention reports (http://tinyurl.com/y6m99xw) that in 2004 there were 6.84 assaults per 1,000 residents in Sweden. For the same year the FBI reports (http://www.fbi.gov/ucr/cius_04/offenses_cleared/index.html) 7.56 assaults per 1,000 residents in the United States. However, in the United States the police cleared 56 percent of all assaults, while only 19 percent were cleared in Sweden. Furthermore, again in 2004 Swedish police removed an average of 61 percent of reported crimes from their logs as "no crime established" – in some police districts as much as 90 percent of all crimes are removed from the logs this way,

without any attempt whatsoever to investigate them (http://svt.se/svt/jsp/ Crosslink.jsp?d=22620&a=290763). The reason is serious shortage of staff. This has the effect of artificially lowering the number of incidents classified as crimes. It is therefore reasonable to adjust the Swedish crime rate to make it methodologically more comparable to the American crime rate. One way of doing this is to estimate the crime rate if Sweden had the same crime solving rate as America. As for assaults, this means an increase in the number of crimes per 1,000 residents from 6.84 to 20. This also goes well with the crime victim rate that the Swedish National Board of Crime Prevention has reported.

135. *TV4 News Station*,4/27/2009: http://www.nyhetskanalen.se/1.967369

136. *Goteborgs-Posten*, 1/31/2010: http://www.gp.se/nyheter/goteborg/1.300677-sjukhus-rapporterar-om-okat-vald

137. *Dagens Nyheter*, 3/8/2010: http://www.dn.se/sthlm/soderort-toppar-ranstatistiken-1.1057676

138. *Kvalls-Posten*, 3/7/2010: http://kvp.expressen.se/nyheter/1.1908619/9-000-anmalda-brott-mot-barn-under-2009

139. *Aftonbladet*, 11/9/2009: http://www.aftonbladet.se/nyheter/article6089900.ab

140. *Goteborgs-Tidningen*; 8/20/2009: http://gt.expressen.se/nyheter/1.1677218/fler-bilar-i-brand-pa-hisingen-i-natt

141. *Upsala Nya Tidning*, 8/29/2009, print edition. An online article was previously available at: http://www.unt.se/avd/1,1826,MC=77-AV_ID=949094,00.html

142. *Goteborgs-Tidningen*, 8/29//2009: http://gt.expressen.se/nyheter/1.1687344/brandman-skadade-i-stenattack-i-natt

143. *Upsala Nya Tidning*, 8/4/2009, print edition. An online article was previously available at: http://www2.unt.se/pages/1,1826,MC=77-AV_ID=939636,00.html?from=puff

144. *Upsala Nya Tidning*, 9/7/2009, print edition. An online article was previously available at: http://www2.unt.se/avd/1,1826,MC=77-AV_ID=953304,00.html?

145. *Sydsvenska Dagbladet*, 9/21/2009: http://sydsvenskan.se/malmo/article551601/Vag-av-vald-pa-kyrkogarden.html and http://sydsvenskan.se/malmo/article551606/Jag-satter-inte-min-fot-pa-Ostra-kyrkogarden-igen.html.

146. Please see: http://preview.bloomberg.com/news/2010-06-10/new-jersey-towns-are-raising-property-taxes-above-christie-s-proposed-cap.html